Jamie Oliver

by Stephanie Watson

LUCENT BOOKS
A part of Gale, Cengage Learning

Detroit • New York • San Francisco • New Haven, Conn • Waterville, Maine • London

LIBRARY OF CONGRESS CATALOGING-IN-PUBLICATION DATA

Watson, Stephanie, 1969-
Jamie Oliver / by Stephanie Watson.
pages cm. -- (People in the news)
Includes bibliographical references and index.
ISBN 978-1-4205-0886-4 (hardback)
1. Oliver, Jamie, 1975---Juvenile literature. 2. Cooks--Great Britain--Biography--Juvenile literature. 3. Restaurateurs--Great Britain--Biography--Juvenile literature. 4. Television personalities--Great Britain--Biography--Juvenile literature. 5. Food habits--Great Britain--Juvenile literature. I. Title.
TX649.O435W38 2013
641.5092--dc23
[B]

2013028451

Lucent Books
27500 Drake Rd.
Farmington Hills, MI 48331

ISBN-13: 978-1-4205-0886-4
ISBN-10: 1-4205-0886-5

Printed in the United States of America
1 2 3 4 5 6 7 17 16 15 14 13

Contents

Foreword

Fame and celebrity are alluring. People are drawn to those who walk in fame's spotlight, whether they are known for great accomplishments or for notorious deeds. The lives of the famous pique public interest and attract attention, perhaps because their experiences seem in some ways so different from, yet in other ways so similar to, our own.

Newspapers, magazines, and television regularly capitalize on this fascination with celebrity by running profiles of famous people. For example, television programs such as *Entertainment Tonight* devote all their programming to stories about entertainment and entertainers. Magazines such as People fill their pages with stories of the private lives of famous people. Even newspapers, newsmagazines, and television news frequently delve into the lives of well-known personalities. Despite the number of articles and programs, few provide more than a superficial glimpse at their subjects.

Lucent's People in the News series offers young readers a deeper look into the lives of today's newsmakers, the influences that have shaped them, and the impact they have had in their fields of endeavor and on other people's lives. The subjects of the series hail from many disciplines and walks of life. They include authors, musicians, athletes, political leaders, entertainers, entrepreneurs, and others who have made a mark on modern life and who, in many cases, will continue to do so for years to come.

These biographies are more than factual chronicles. Each book emphasizes the contributions, accomplishments, or deeds that have brought fame or notoriety to the individual and shows how that person has influenced modern life. Authors portray their subjects in a realistic, unsentimental light. For example, Bill Gates—cofounder of the software giant Microsoft—has been instrumental in making personal computers the most vital tool of the modern age. Few dispute his business savvy, his perseverance, or his technical expertise, yet critics say he is ruthless in his dealings with competitors and driven more by his desire to maintain Microsoft's dominance in the computer industry than by an interest in furthering technology.

In these books, young readers will encounter inspiring stories about real people who achieved success despite enormous obstacles. Oprah Winfrey—one of the most powerful, most watched, and wealthiest women in television history—spent the first six years of her life in the care of her grandparents while her unwed mother sought work and a better life elsewhere. Her adolescence was colored by pregnancy at age fourteen, rape, and sexual abuse.

Each author documents and supports his or her work with an array of primary and secondary source quotations taken from diaries, letters, speeches, and interviews. All quotes are footnoted to show readers exactly how and where biographers derive their information and provide guidance for further research. The quotations enliven the text by giving readers eyewitness views of the life and accomplishments of each person covered in the People in the News series.

In addition, each book in the series includes photographs, annotated bibliographies, timelines, and comprehensive indexes. For both the casual reader and the student researcher, the People in the News series offers insight into the lives of today's newsmakers—people who shape the way we live, work, and play in the modern age.

The Crusade Against Turkey Twizzlers

It was 2005, and Jamie Oliver was furious. The British chef and cooking show star had built his career on preparing good-quality foods made with simple, healthy ingredients. Now he had taken a look inside his country's school lunchrooms and was appalled at what he found there. The kids were gorging themselves on fattening, unhealthy food such as french fries, burgers, pizza, and sodas. They were doing so at a time when one-third of Britain's population was struggling with obesity. One food in particular that was offered on school menus really got Oliver fuming: Turkey Twizzlers.

Turkey Twizzlers are a spiral-shaped twirl of processed turkey meat. They had become a staple on school lunch menus in England, even though they contain unhealthy ingredients such as pork fat, wheat starch, artificial sweeteners, hydrogenated vegetable oil, and artificial flavorings. Turkey Twizzlers are made up of more than 21 percent fat—which is twice the recommended amount for processed meats in Great Britain. To Oliver, Turkey Twizzlers were the perfect symbol of the sorry state that British school lunch programs were in.

Using His Influence

As a celebrity chef who had championed cooking with healthy ingredients for nearly a decade, Oliver thought he was in a unique position to make Britain's school lunch programs healthier. At just thirty years old, he already had a string of hit television shows, including *The Naked Chef* and *Jamie's Kitchen*, and a series of best-selling books related to those shows. His programs had been broadcast in a hundred countries; his books translated into more than thirty languages. He had launched a charity called Fifteen to train at-risk youths to be chefs. The endeavor was so successful that he franchised it in several different cities throughout the United Kingdom (UK) and around the world.

Typically when Oliver had a message to get across, people watched and listened—something that he had learned a few years earlier when his first series, *The Naked Chef*, became a huge hit. "I would make focaccia [an Italian-style bread] with semolina [a type of wheat flour] on the show, and semolina would sell out across the country," he said. "You quickly learn that you have a responsibility."[1] Oliver now felt that his responsibility was to crusade against unhealthy eating and to overhaul his country's school meals.

After focusing his attention on schools in his home country, Oliver turned his attention to the United States, where he lobbied for healthier menu options and taught cafeteria workers healthy food preparation techniques. Despite Oliver's best intentions, his input was not always welcome. In both the UK and the United States, he met with a lot of resistance. In Los Angeles, for example, school officials banned him from getting anywhere near school cafeterias. Some critics claimed Oliver was just exploiting the childhood obesity problem to gain attention for his shows. Others, however, viewed him as sincere and appreciated that he was trying to change eating habits for the better. "He is a rebel chef who genuinely cares about food and nutritional standards and for that he should be applauded,"[2] wrote a commentator in the *Lancet* medical journal.

A Genuine Love of Food

One thing that can never be argued about Oliver is his genuine love of food. "Food is my hobby, my job, my life,"[3] he says. "I like to eat everything. It doesn't matter to me if it's not my style. It's all an education to me."[4] He has always been passionate about cooking and food education, because it has allowed him to feel a sense of discovery every single day. "When I've found a new dish or tried out a new technique in cooking, I get the same feeling as when I first learned to ride a bike,"[5] he says.

Oliver has built his career on the idea of taking food back to its basics. "I believe in simple cooking and simple serving,"[6] he says. It is Oliver's sincerity and his ability to convey his real love for food that has made him so popular with audiences. "He's not famous because of his food," notes Jay Rayner of the British newspaper the *Guardian*. "He's famous because he's an extraordinarily

Jamie Oliver's love of food led him to revolutionize school lunch programs around the world, open restaurants, write books, and host his own cooking programs on television.

good communicator. . . . Unlike other people in the food world he is not a fake."[7]

Oliver has stayed grounded and real, despite his rise to fame and the fortune that has come along with it. That down-to-earth quality—along with his love of good cooking and his crusade against products like Turkey Twizzlers—are qualities that have made him a globally recognized chef, entrepreneur, and social issues advocate.

Chapter 1

Pint-Sized Chef

Clavering, Essex, is a picturesque little English village, one of many similarly quaint villages that dot the eastern part of England. The town lies just 40 miles (64km) northeast of the bustling capital city of London, but its rolling green hills, thatched cottages, and medieval church make Clavering appear as if it rose straight out of a much earlier time period. It feels hundreds of years old, far removed from modern civilization.

One of the village's institutions is an inn and pub called the Cricketers, which has been in business since the sixteenth century. With its brick interior, roaring hearth, and beamed ceilings, the Cricketers, similar to the town in which it resides, is a throwback to a time when King Henry VIII ruled England.

The Cricketers is one of many historic pubs in England, yet it has one notable distinction: The kitchen of this pub is where celebrity chef Jamie Oliver first donned an apron and fell in love with the art of cooking.

What's in a Name?

Jamie Oliver was born in Clavering on May 27, 1975, to parents Trevor and Sally Oliver. His first name—which is usually a nickname for James—was given somewhat by mistake. "It was supposed to be James but my Dad got it wrong when he got my papers signed when I was born,"[8] Oliver says. Nevertheless, Oliver considers his father his hero, because he is "a self-made man, hard-working, honest."[9]

In 1976, not long after Jamie's birth, his mother became pregnant with his sister, Anna-Marie. With young Jamie in tow and another child on the way, the Olivers decided to take over the Cricketers and make it their own. The place was in terrible shape when they arrived, and the young couple did not have much money for repairs and renovations. In fact, just for the couple to be able to buy the pub, Trevor's father had to guarantee the loan (that is, he promised to make the payments if Trevor could not afford them).

In a way, Trevor Oliver was born to own and manage a pub. He had been raised in his parents' pub, the Plough and Sail, in Paglesham, a parish (part of a county) in Essex. Trevor had trained as a chef at Southend Catering College, as well as in Switzerland and at the French restaurant A L'Ecu de France, in London. After completing his culinary training, Trevor, along with his new wife, Sally, ran a pub in South Ockendon (a town about 22 miles [35km] east of London). It was called the Prince of Wales, and the couple managed it for two years. Trevor ran the kitchen, while Sally worked the front of the house and

A smiling Trevor Oliver stands in front of the Cricketers pub, which he bought in the late 1970s. A young Jamie spent a lot of time in the pub's kitchen, which is where his love of cooking began.

A History of Clavering, England

Clavering, like many English villages, has been in existence for centuries. There is still evidence of Roman roads meandering through the town—indicating that the Romans had a settlement there. The town was first given the name "Claefring" in the eleventh century, which over time morphed into "Clavering."

Clavering features a medieval church, as well as the ruins of a moated castle, which may be the oldest castle site in eastern England. Though the town prospered during the time of the Tudors (the royal house of King Henry VIII and Queen Elizabeth I), by the 1800s, Clavering had fallen into poverty. However, in the following century it experienced a revival as London commuters bought homes and settled there.

Even as Clavering has embraced the twenty-first century, it has carefully preserved its history. Today, the village looks very much like it did five hundred years ago, dotted with cottages, churches, and pubs.

handled the bookkeeping (she had worked in a London bank before marrying Trevor). Once they took over the Cricketers, the couple assumed the same roles. Trevor managed the kitchen while Sally ran the business end of the operation.

A Huckleberry Finn Childhood

Jamie has described his childhood as similar to that of the characters in *Huckleberry Finn*, the Mark Twain novel about the adventures of two young boys—Tom Sawyer and Huckleberry Finn—along the Mississippi River. If Oliver was Tom Sawyer, then his pal Jimmy Doherty was Huckleberry Finn. "He lived next to the River Stort so as kids we would be found mucking about down at the river, fishing, trying to build rafts, building tree houses, dens,"[10] he remembers.

Their outings often involved causing mischief—even if inadvertently. For example, one evening after they had been out fishing, the boys left their boat and fishing gear and went to get some dinner. They did not realize that Doherty had forgotten to put the lid back on the pot of maggots they had been using as bait. When they returned to the boat, they found a woman standing there "screaming her heart out."[11] The boys looked down to see maggots crawling all over their boat.

Along with fishing and playing outside with friends, Jamie was very interested in music. Classical, jazz, punk—he loved it all. He listened to the British pop band Five Star and idolized Steve Gadd—a legendary drummer who performed with artists such as Paul Simon and Aretha Franklin. In 1989 at age fourteen, Jamie started drumming in his own band, called Scarlet Division.

Growing Up on Pub Food

Food and his family's pub were also important parts of Jamie's childhood. "I never realized how lucky I was growing up in my parents' pub until I was older," he notes. "They served proper British food, always made from fresh ingredients, cooked from scratch by cooks who cared."[12] When he was not outside playing (or causing mischief) with his friends, Jamie could be found in the pub's kitchen, eagerly watching the chefs work. Sometimes the chefs staged a race with the live lobsters or crabs, and Jamie cheered on the crustaceans as they scuttled toward a finish line.

On Sunday nights, the Oliver family gathered for dinner at the Cricketers. Aunts, uncles, grandparents, and cousins all sat around the table together. "Those dinners were a lot of fun," Sally Oliver recalls. "The kids would always prod my husband to make some sort of speech or toast. You know, 'Lovely to have you all here gathered around the table.' That sort of thing. Well, the kids would egg him on, he'd start to get all emotional, and then the kids would laugh and laugh."[13] The dinners were usually boisterous affairs, and Jamie loved them. He especially loved the food. Although his mother was not a professional chef, she was a talented amateur. "My mum's Sunday Roast is still my favorite meal of all time,"[14] he claims. The hearty meal of pub fare usually ended with a big, rich pudding for dessert, also made by his mother.

Unlike many children, who crave french fries, pizza, and burgers, Jamie loved to sample new, and often exotic, foods. "I remember that Jamie was quite an easy child to feed," says his mother. "He always wanted to try different things, especially anything unusual that he had seen prepared in the kitchen."[15] For example, he loved smoked salmon drizzled with lemon juice, and he savored the liver sausages his mother packed in his school lunch.

Eating was also central to the family's vacations, which they often shared with friends. Once a year, the Olivers got together with the family of Jamie's pal Jimmy Doherty. They—along with other friends—rented boats and vacationed together in the Norfolk Broads, a series of rivers and lakes near the eastern coast of England that is a popular holiday spot for people living in the region.

On these trips, Sally Oliver often bought local fruits and vegetables and used the meager cooking facilities on the boat to whip up fabulous feasts for her family and guests. "With limited kit [kitchen facilities] we'd make anything pot-based—Bolognese [a meat-based pasta sauce], curries, cottage pie [a meat pie with a crust made from mashed potatoes], chicken pie,"[16] her son remembers.

Cooking on a Chair

By age eight, Jamie was already clamoring to help out in the pub's kitchen. "I decided that most of the hard-core action was in the kitchen with the real men, and that's where I wanted to be,"[17] he writes in his book *The Naked Chef*. Jamie started out performing the lowliest task—washing dishes. From there, he was allowed to do some basic cooking chores, such as peeling potatoes and shelling peas. By age eleven, he could julienne (cut into thin strips) vegetables as quickly as any professional chef in

Oliver loved the food at Cricketers and looked forward to dinner there every Sunday night with his family.

the pub's kitchen. Jamie's sister also worked at the pub, but she waited tables.

Even at an early age Jamie was determined to get the craft of cooking right—starting with making the perfect omelet, the first thing his mother taught him how to cook. "I was fascinated by making proper omelets, and for a couple of years that's all I did!"[18] he says. Despite his focus, Jamie was still a child and thus had limitations in the kitchen. "We used to stand him on a chair so that he could reach the work surface," remembers his mother, "and obviously he used to get into a real mess."[19]

After mastering basic cooking skills, Jamie went on to concoct his own pizza recipes for his friends. "I remember thinking they were excellent, but they were horrible!"[20] he recalls. To further his culinary education, Jamie sought help from the pub's chefs, who were happy to instruct the young chef-in-training.

Working in the kitchen was not only a fun and educational endeavor for Jamie—it was also lucrative. He wanted to have an allowance, just as many of his friends had, but when he asked his father to give him some pocket money, Trevor Oliver replied, "No, but you can get up in the morning and *earn* some if you want!"[21] His father was determined that Jamie work hard both in the kitchen and around the house to earn his allowance—and that included working on weekends. As a teenager, if Jamie ever overslept on a Saturday morning, he was awakened by a splash of cold water from the garden hose, which his father aimed straight through Jamie's bedroom window. This rude awakening was Trevor's way of telling his son it was time to get up and do his chores.

As Jamie got older, he was given more responsibility in the Cricketers' kitchen. "We had chefs working in the kitchen who gave easy jobs to him and I think it made him feel really grown up—he thought he was 'one of the boys,'"[22] his mother says. By age fourteen, Jamie was already a fairly accomplished chef.

Young Jamie's first cooking task was to chop vegetables—a skill he mastered at the age of eleven.

The Cricketers

Jamie Oliver developed his love of cooking from growing up in his parents' pub, the Cricketers, surrounded by the sights, smells, and tastes of food. The Cricketers has a long history in the town of Clavering. The fourteen-room inn and pub has been housing weary travelers and serving up traditional English meals since the sixteenth century.

In a country that has long been criticized for its lack of good food, the Cricketers gained a reputation for using fresh ingredients and homemade recipes. Visitors who have posted reviews on the website TripAdvisor have praised the pub's "excellent food and service." Trevor and Sally Oliver bought the pub in 1976, and they still own and run it today. Their inn has won four stars (out of five) and a Silver Award from the English Tourist Board.

Quoted in TripAdvisor. "The Cricketers (Clavering)." www.tripadvisor.co.uk/Hotel_Review-g2690291-d269671-Reviews-The_Cricketers-Clavering_Saffron_Walden_Essex_England.html.

He was quick with his knife skills, and he knew how to cook a large number of meals for a dining room full of people. Sometimes he helped the other chefs cook a hundred or more meals in a single night.

Trouble in School

Cooking was the one thing Jamie felt he could do well. He struggled through his classes at school due to dyslexia, a learning disorder that made it nearly impossible for him to read words and letters correctly. "People just thought I was thick [slow-learning]. It was a struggle,"[23] he says.

Put in a special-needs class in Clavering Primary School, the elementary school in his town, Jamie was bored with the slow-paced program and frustrated by his lack of progress in school.

Instead of focusing on his studies, Jamie earned a reputation as a mischief maker. Whenever the special-needs teacher went to the bathroom, he and the other nine students in the class would wad up pieces of paper and throw them out the window at the people below. His sense of humor, along with his popularity, size, and toughness, prevented Jamie from getting teased about being in a special-needs class. "I was one of the bigger boys and if anyone had offended me by calling me special needs, I would have given them a slap,"[24] he says.

Schoolwork was not the only thing that gave Jamie trouble. He also had a terrible time with girls. "I wasn't very confident. My voice shook when I talked to girls,"[25] he confesses. When he met a beautiful girl named Juliette "Jools" Norton, Jamie could barely muster the courage to speak to her. Instead, he just avoided her. She did not pay him much attention. "But a year and half later—I don't know why—she had a change of heart. She decided she quite liked me. And as soon as I found out I was all over it like a rash,"[26] he says. For their first date, Jamie and Jools went to the movies on a double date with his friend Jimmy Doherty and another girl. Jamie was the only one with a car—a Ford Fiesta. On their way to the movies, Jamie accidentally smashed into the back of another car. After that incident, he was convinced that Jools only went out with him again because she felt sorry for him. "She thought, 'the way he drives, he needs support in life,'"[27] he quips.

Jamie did not have a lot of extra time for dating, because he spent his weekends throughout the school year working at the Cricketers. In the summers, he further improved his cooking skills at the Starr restaurant, a well-respected eatery in Great Dunmow, about 15 miles (24km) away from his home in Clavering. First he was assigned a basic cooking task—making cold appetizers. But within a few weeks, he had taken over the responsibilities of a chef twice his age, making full meals.

Jamie's gift for cooking, and his love for sharing the foods he made with other people, were evident, even as a teenager. One summer afternoon, he made smoked salmon sandwiches for his friends—one of whom initially balked at this menu choice. "He really didn't want to eat it, and then, when he did, he wouldn't eat anything else all summer," recalls Jamie. "That's when I understood how powerful food can be."[28]

Off to Culinary School

In 1991 Jamie's dyslexia became a severe obstacle for him. After struggling through his studies at Newport Free Grammar School (where he attended middle school and high school), Jamie had had enough of traditional education. He dropped out at age sixteen to attend Westminster Catering College (now called Westminster Kingsway College) in London. The college offers a variety of courses to train chefs de cuisine and pastry chefs. Two other celebrity British chefs—Antony Worrall Thompson and Ainsley Harriott—also attended Westminster several years before Jamie arrived.

For three years, Jamie commuted to and from London to complete his culinary training. "I was completely in awe of the

Oliver left grammar school to attend Westminster Catering College (now Westminster Kingsway College) in London.

enormous college and the cosmopolitan mix of students,"[29] he recalls. While attending Westminster, Jamie befriended a fellow student named Marco, who was Italian. Through Marco, Jamie fell in love with pasta and other Italian foods. Yet after graduation he did not travel to Italy but to France to further develop his talents in the kitchen. Jamie wanted to learn more about food preparation, and he knew that France was the best place to do it. Accomplished chefs around the world use French cooking techniques, such as flambé (pouring liquor over a dish and igniting it) and chiffonade (cutting herbs and leafy green vegetables into thin strips).

Jamie might not have gotten a traditional education, but he had mastered the skills he needed to make him a world-class chef. He would take those culinary talents to two of the most respected restaurants in London—and get discovered by a TV producer in the process.

Chapter 2

Discovery in the Kitchen

After graduating from Westminster Catering College, Oliver continued his training by spending a summer at Chateau Tilques in northern France. The elegant hotel has been in existence since the late 1800s, and its restaurant, Le Vert Mesnil, is highly respected in the region.

Working under the restaurant's master chefs, Oliver discovered that a lot more than meat, vegetables, and seasonings go into creating fine French cuisine. "It wasn't until I went to work at Chateau Tilques in France that I learnt that quality, real care, love and individual flair have to go into every stage of food preparation,"[30] Oliver says.

The three months he spent at Chateau Tilques transformed him. He was very impressed by the work ethic of the chefs he trained with. He returned to England a chef obsessed with finding the freshest and finest ingredients.

Studying with a Master Bread and Pasta Maker

Oliver considered where he could go after cooking at one of the finest establishments in France. During his college days, one of his teachers had asked everyone in the class what they wanted to do after graduating. Most of the students said their intention was to cook at restaurants like Le Manoir aux Quat'Saisons and the Ritz—England's finest French restaurants—but not Oliver.

"I just put my hand up and said, 'I want to learn how to make really good bread and pasta.'"[31] When Oliver told Marco about his intention, his friend replied, "If you want to make good bread, go and see Gennaro."[32]

"Gennaro" is Gennaro Contaldo, the Italian-born chef who had made a name for himself at some of London's most popular Italian eateries. In the early 1990s, Contaldo worked at Neal Street Restaurant in London's historic Covent Garden district. Neal Street, owned by Italian restaurateur Antonio Carluccio, was well known for its pastas and breads. It was the perfect match for Oliver's interests. At age nineteen, he signed on as

Determined to make good bread and pasta, Oliver sought out chef Gennaro Contaldo. After much prodding, the chef agreed to help Oliver prep his bread recipes at the restaurant in which the two worked.

Neal Street

For nearly three decades, Chef Antonio Carluccio's Neal Street Restaurant was a focal point in London's upscale Covent Garden district. English designer Sir Terence Conran founded the restaurant in the early 1970s. Back then, Neal Street existed to feed employees and clients of Conran's design business on the floor above.

In 1981 Italian chef Antonio Carluccio took over the kitchen. By 1989 he owned the restaurant. Carluccio turned Neal Street into one of the city's most celebrated Italian restaurants. Celebrities and dignitaries from Prince Charles to Sir Elton John flocked there for its authentic cuisine.

As Carluccio became famous across England, he launched a chain of cafés and delicatessens. In 2007 the iconic restaurant came to an end, forced to close its doors by developers who had purchased the land. Neal Street Restaurant served its last meal on March 17, 2007.

the restaurant's pastry chef because it was the only job available there at the time.

At first, Carluccio would not let Oliver anywhere near his star chef. So Oliver went straight to Contaldo himself. "I said to him: 'Gennaro—I keep asking if I can come and help you make bread in the night and they keep saying no.' Contaldo said: 'It's because they think you're going to steal my bread recipe.'"[33] Oliver had no intention of stealing Contaldo's recipes, and he refused to take no for an answer.

Because he was the new guy in the kitchen, Oliver had to work a late shift, which kept him at the restaurant until one o'clock in the morning. Contaldo worked the early shift, coming into the restaurant just an hour later. Oliver was determined to learn Contaldo's preparation techniques. So during the hour in between their shifts, he decided he would try to get on Contaldo's good side.

An Extremely Hard Worker

Oliver began prepping the elder chef's bread ingredients so that Contaldo could sleep in at home for an extra hour. By the time Contaldo arrived each day, Oliver had already weighed out the flour and heated up the ovens for him. His efforts worked. Contaldo finally agreed to let Oliver watch him prepare the bread and pasta.

To learn everything he could about bread and pasta making, Oliver picked up a second shift. After finishing his regular shift each day, he trained with Contaldo from 3:00 to 7:00 A.M. Oliver did that for several months, until his father noticed he looked sick from working so hard. But the result was worth the long hours. Contaldo made Oliver his protégé. Contaldo was a strict teacher, but he became a role model for Oliver. "He was like my second father,"[34] Oliver says. "I learned everything from Gennaro—heart, soul, romance, fantasy—every nice word you can say."[35]

Oliver was only at Neal Street Restaurant for a year, but it was long enough to learn how to be a master bread and pasta maker—which is what he had set out to do. By the time he left, Oliver already had big dreams. Contaldo recalls Oliver saying to him, "'I'm going to open my own restaurant and one day you can work for me.' I laughed. Then he said, 'Not one restaurant, but restaurants all around the country, all over the world.'"[36]

The River Café

In 1996 Oliver took his Italian cooking skills to a new job at the River Café. The restaurant is appropriately named—it sits along the banks of the Thames River in west London. Chef-owners Rose Gray and Ruth Rogers started the River Café together in 1987, when English cuisine was best known for boiled potatoes and fried fish. In opening the River Café, Gray and Rogers wanted to recreate the kind of fresh, farmhouse cooking they had enjoyed when they traveled to the Tuscany region of Italy—foods like Tuscan bread soup, lamb with rosemary and garlic, and grilled polenta (a side dish made from cornmeal).

By the time Oliver arrived, the restaurant had earned its place among London's top Italian eateries. The café had a Michelin star—one of the highest honors a restaurant can receive for its cuisine. The owners were serious about their food—they flew in fresh ingredients from all over Europe (including butter, cheese, and white peaches from Italy). But they were never pretentious. "What Rose Gray and Ruth Rogers have done is create a deceptively simple style that makes a virtue of food which is free of disguise or complication," a columnist at London's *Independent* newspaper writes of the River Café's owners. "By using only the very best and freshest ingredients, the two of them have transformed and elevated what is essentially home cooking."[37]

Oliver was inspired by his employers' straightforward approach to good cooking. "They are not cliché chefs, not 'cheffy' in the slightest. They have passion,"[38] he says. During his nearly four years at the River Café, he became even more convinced that it takes scrupulous attention to ingredients to make a delicious meal. "Those two ladies taught me all about the time and

Oliver began working for Rose Gray at the River Café in west London. He appreciated the chef's love of simple, yet delicious, food using only the freshest ingredients.

effort that goes into creating the freshest, most honest, totally delicious food,"[39] Oliver says.

His work at the River Café helped Oliver develop the culinary technique that would soon define him as a chef. Yet he honed that technique unintentionally at home. When he first moved to London, Oliver rented a flat (the British word for apartment) in Hampstead. It was a very expensive part of the city, and Oliver did not earn much money at the time. He could only afford a tiny flat—with an equally tiny kitchen. Eventually he moved into a basement flat in the district of Hammersmith, which was closer to the River Café; however, its kitchen was not any bigger.

Cooking in such tiny accommodations forced Oliver to create simplified versions of the meals he prepared at the River Café. "I found myself stripping down those recipes to something quite basic," he writes. "I then adapted them, using what I did have in the cupboard, larder, fridge or garden."[40] He came to realize that simple was not bad—actually, the food he prepared with minimal ingredients and basic cooking techniques was quite tasty. He used this idea to amass a collection of simple, delicious, yet easy-to-prepare recipes that would form the foundation of his culinary career.

A Life-Changing Holiday Special

In 1997 the River Café was one of London's most celebrated restaurants. So when producers at the BBC television network were looking for a place to film their Christmas cooking special, they called Rogers and Gray. The result was a documentary called *Christmas at the River Café*.

The show centered on Rogers and Gray. As the cameras rolled, the two women whipped up a holiday meal, complete with mincemeat pies (a traditional English holiday pie made from chopped dried fruit, spices, and liquor). Behind them viewers could spot a fresh-faced young chef with mussed blondish hair and chubby cheeks, who chopped vegetables and stirred the contents of saucepans with seemingly boundless energy.

Since Oliver's television debut in 1997 on* Christmas at the River Café*, his career has taken off with a variety of television shows and books. Here, he cooks with actor Robin Williams on NBC's* Today*.

Although Oliver was in the background, he pretty much stole the show as he bustled about the kitchen and asked the camera crew to move out of his way. Interestingly, Oliver was not even supposed to be at work that day. He was filling in for another chef who was sick.

The day after the special aired, the River Café's phone rang off the hook. The callers were not trying to make a reservation.

"In Defence of English Cooking"

In his essay "In Defence of English Cooking," English novelist George Orwell wrote, "It is commonly said, even by the English themselves, that English cooking is the worst in the world." British cooking earned its poor culinary reputation by cranking out centuries worth of gloppy porridges, overfried fish, and soggy boiled meats.

Yet it was also the English who pioneered classic comfort fare—a diverse mix of savory puddings, pies, and stews. The English also invented the sandwich and infused it with a bit of elegance by cutting off the crusts and presenting it on fine china at high tea. Through the process of immigration, Britain also became a melting pot of foreign cuisines—including samosas and masalas from India and spicy Szechuan dishes and dim sum from China.

The English invented the sandwich and added a little elegance by cutting off crusts and serving with tea.

Over the last few decades, British cooking has progressed even further. Today, London's restaurants rank among the finest in the world. Celebrity chefs like Nigella Lawson, Gordon Ramsay, and Jamie Oliver have proven that the Brits can produce much more sophisticated fare than just fish and chips.

George Orwell. "In Defence of English Cooking." In *As I Please, 1943–1946,* edited by Sonia Orwell and Ian Angus. Boston: David R. Godine, 2000, p. 38.

They were looking for Oliver. "I got calls from five production companies . . . companies all wanting to talk about a possible show," Oliver recalls. "I couldn't believe it and thought it was my mates [friends] winding me up [playing a joke on him]!"[41] He was so convinced it was his friends calling, that he was verbally nasty to one caller. Then he realized that the caller was "using words like commission and pilot, which were far too intelligent and underground for my boys."[42]

Fortunately, he was not nasty to Patricia Llewellyn, a producer at Optomen Television, a production company. Llewellyn already had a hit cooking series called *Two Fat Ladies* (starring heavy-set English cooks Jennifer Paterson and Clarissa Dickson Wright). In the offbeat show, the "two fat ladies" roared across the English countryside on a motorcycle and sidecar. They cooked old-fashioned comfort foods full of butter, lard, and cream. When Llewellyn watched *Christmas at the River Café*, Oliver's hip look and charisma "shone out like a beacon,"[43] she says. "He was doing spinach in the background and he seemed so young. This little baby face and these great big worker's hands."[44]

Llewellyn had a big proposition for the twenty-one-year-old chef. She wanted to give him his own television series. In just a couple of years, Oliver would go from behind the scenes to the center of attention.

Chapter 3

Becoming the Naked Chef

After negotiating with Llewellyn, Oliver signed on to host a new BBC television cooking series, with him as the star. The big question was what to call the show. The producers wanted to give it an attention-grabbing title. They passed around a number of silly names, such as *Forking Gorgeous*. Then one member of the production team suggested *The Naked Chef*.

The Naked Chef Is Born

The new show's title did not mean that Oliver would be cooking in the nude (although it was meant to suggest just that); it referred to how the chef's ingredients and cooking techniques were stripped down to their bare essentials. Because of its provocative nature, Oliver hated the name. "Tacky,"[45] was his gut reaction. He was afraid his mother would think he was starring in a dirty program. To avoid any confusion about his apparel (or lack thereof), the show's opening segment featured a clip of Oliver saying, "No way! It's not me—it's the food."[46]

Oliver might not have approved of the show's title, but he had more control over its look and content. He chose a hip dance music soundtrack for the show's opener, which also played behind the noncooking segments—such as when he was riding his scooter around town. He also decided on a loose, handheld camera style. Above all, he made sure that episodes featured him cooking the kind of food he loved. The recipes he shared with his viewers were not fancy, but they were made with the best-quality ingredients. "Even though I'm a young boy, I have a lot of integrity," he said about the show. "We're not doing crappy, shallow food."[47] Sticking to his culinary roots, Oliver displayed his talent for making simple, hearty Italian fare—homemade pastas, sauces, and fresh meats and fish.

The title* The Naked Chef *referred to how Oliver's ingredients and cooking techniques were stripped down to their bare essentials, not that Oliver was cooking in the nude. Initially, the chef did not like the title because of its implication.

***Many of Oliver's friends and family appeared on the show, including girlfriend Jools Norton. Norton later became a production assistant on* The Naked Chef.**

Making *The Naked Chef*

In 1999 the show began filming at a house on Chequer Street in London. To keep the feel of the series authentic, Oliver moved into the property so he could cook in his own kitchen. Shots of him sliding down the banister of the home's spiral staircase and riding out the front door on his scooter became regular features of the show. With his cool vibe, Cockney accent (a working-class London accent), mussed hair, and old jeans, Oliver was the antidote to the stodgy cooking programs that often aired on British television. "There weren't any young people on TV," Oliver says. "It was like you had to be an old git [bum] to do it."[48]

Adding to the authenticity, the show featured Oliver's real-life friends, family members, and even his former mentor, Gennaro

Contaldo. When he cooked a meal in front of the camera, his friends and family gathered around the table to eat it. Oliver's longtime girlfriend, Jools Norton, lived with him and also appeared on the show. In one episode of the series, she arrived home to discover that Oliver had cooked her a romantic meal of broiled fish and a chocolate tart (he earned a kiss for his efforts). Eventually, Norton, who had worked as a model, became a production assistant on the show so that she could spend more time with Oliver.

The point of *The Naked Chef* was that foods cooked with just a few basic ingredients can be delicious and that anyone—from stay-at-home-moms to kids—has the ability to cook well. In keeping with Oliver's bubbly personality, *The Naked Chef* took a lighthearted, unconventional approach to cooking. In one episode, Oliver made spaghetti while babysitting for his three young cousins. In another, he cooked breakfast on the beach for some Australian friends who were teaching him how to surf.

As a first-time TV show host, Oliver was far from polished at the start. He often had to be prompted by director/producer Llewellyn from off camera. She would ask questions about ingredients or cooking techniques to keep him talking. Eventually he became more comfortable on camera and needed less offscreen prompting.

Despite Oliver's personality, the show almost did not get aired on British TV at all. "When I delivered *The Naked Chef* to the BBC they didn't like it, and it sat on the shelf for five months," says Llewellyn. Finally, the network premiered the show in the spring of 1999. Even then, it took a while for viewers to catch on. "It wasn't until the last few programmes that the figures exploded,"[49] she adds.

The figures she was referring to were the show's ratings, which propelled Oliver to fame within a few months of *The Naked Chef's* premiere. Viewers could not get enough of Oliver, but critics had mixed reviews. Although they admired his approachable style, they were not sold on his simplistic approach to cooking. "We love Jamie Oliver for lots of reasons," wrote a reviewer at the *Guardian*, a major British newspaper, "[but] his technical ability as a cook is not one of them."[50]

On a Roll

Regardless of what some critics thought, by 2000, the twenty-five-year-old chef was on a roll. His show was a huge hit. It was nominated for a British Academy of Film and Television Arts (BAFTA) Award (similar to the Oscars and Emmys in the United States). The BBC commissioned a second, and then a third season of the series.

The Naked Chef spawned several best-selling cookbooks, each packed with Oliver's favorite recipes. The books were designed to teach amateur chefs how to cook dishes such as the perfect roast chicken or homemade ravioli. It was daunting for a person with severe dyslexia to write a cookbook—let alone several. "I've always struggled with writing,"[51] admits Oliver. So when it came time to create a book, he supplied the ingenuity and had his editor help with the actual writing. Their collaboration paid off: Published in 2000, *The Naked Chef* cookbook became a huge success, selling more than a million copies worldwide. Sequels to this book included *Happy Days with the Naked Chef* (the number-one-selling nonfiction book in the United Kingdom the year it was published, 2001) and *The Return of the Naked Chef* (2010). The books' success propelled Oliver to fame—he was even invited to 10 Downing Street (the British prime minister's residence and offices) to cook for then–prime minister Tony Blair and visiting foreign dignitaries.

As if a hit television series and best-selling cookbooks were not enough, Oliver started to expand into other food-related ventures. He became chef-consultant to Monte's, an elegant restaurant in the posh Chelsea section of London, where he helped create the restaurant's menu. In 2000 Sainsbury's, a major supermarket chain in England, made Oliver the face of its advertising campaign called "Making Life Taste Better." For a while, commercials featuring Oliver were all over the television. "You couldn't sit down to an episode of *Coronation Street* [a British soap opera] without being exhorted by the cheeky [endearingly impertinent] foodie to buy buffalo mozzarella or lemon thyme,"[52] one reporter wrote. Oliver went on to lead more than a hundred advertising campaigns for the supermarket, including

"Feed Your Family for a Fiver," in which he tried to convince British families they could feed their families an entire meal for just £5 ($7.60).

Oliver's newfound fame did wonders for the supermarket's sales. The first television ad featured Oliver cooking a prawn (large shrimp) curry. After the commercial aired, sales of ingredients used to make prawn curry jumped by 900 percent at

Monte's

By 2000 Jamie Oliver had established himself as the kind of laid-back, down-to-earth guy viewers could imagine themselves hanging out and cooking with. He prided himself on creating simple, basic food that anyone could cook and enjoy. Therefore, many people were surprised when he took a job as consultant to Monte's, an upscale restaurant in London's Chelsea district.

Monte's (which has since closed) appealed to an older, affluent crowd. Diners needed to be able to afford the restaurant's entrees, many of which cost more than £26 ($40). To some reviewers, the formal, wood-and-leather-paneled dining room seemed out of character for someone like Oliver. As one reviewer wrote, "I doubt whether many of those mates of his who crowd into his living room at the end of each programme to eat his grub could afford to come here regularly or, given the location, whether they would want to."[1] Another reviewer remarked that the food at Monte's seemed "gauche" (crude) and "joyless"[2] for someone who had a passion for cooking, such as Oliver. Perhaps because of some of these issues, the partnership did not last long—by 2002 Oliver had moved on to other ventures.

1. Jay Rayner. "Naked Ambition." *Observer* (London), September 16, 2000. www.guardian.co.uk/lifeandstyle/2000/sep/17/foodanddrink.restaurants.
2. Fay Maschler. "Naked Truth About Monte's." *London Evening Standard*, August 15, 2000. www.standard.co.uk/goingout/restaurants/naked-truth-about-montes-7431274.html.

Sainsbury's stores. Sainsbury's claims Oliver increased its sales by as much as 500 percent on other products as well. Oliver did well from the deal, too. He reportedly earned more than £1 million ($1.5 million) a year from it.

The collaboration with Sainsbury's was not only about money, though. Oliver lent his name and face to some good causes, too. He was featured in the supermarket's "Switch the Fish" campaign, for example, which tried to convince shoppers to buy more sustainable fish species—ones that are not being overfished. Other ads urged people to eat more healthfully by buying more nutritious foods at their local Sainsbury's. Oliver also starred in Sainsbury's "Comic Relief" commercial, which was part of a charitable effort to raise money for needy people in Africa and around the world.

British prime minister Tony Blair (center) invited Oliver to cook for him and visiting foreign dignitaries at his 10 Downing Street residence. Here, Oliver looks on as Italian prime minister Massimo D'Alema and Blair admire his cookbook.

The Chef Can Play, Too

Oliver's fame did not only sell supermarket products. It also helped promote one of his earliest projects. When he was fourteen, he and a few friends had formed a band called Scarlet Division, in which Oliver was the drummer. He describes the band's sound as a blend of American country and British alternative "somewhere between Texas, the Pretenders [a 1980s English alternative band] and modern techno [electronic dance music]."[53]

The band had been playing gigs around London since their teens. But the success of *The Naked Chef* got them booked into bigger venues, playing to bigger audiences. Oliver had to start thinking about what might happen to his cooking career if Scarlet Division got a record deal. "It could mean putting the cooking to one side for a while," he said at the time. "But at the moment I am far too busy to worry about record deals—and I could never give up cooking for good."[54] Fortunately for him, Oliver never had to make the choice. In 2000 Scarlet Division hit number forty-two on the British music charts with a song called "Sundial." After that, however, the band fizzled into obscurity, leaving plenty of time for Oliver's cooking shows, books, and corporate endorsements.

The Naked Chef Conquers America—and the World

Buoyed by all of his success, in 2001 Oliver took his cooking show on the road. He launched the Happy Days Live tour, in which he traveled all over Great Britain cooking live for tens of thousands of people who packed into theaters to watch him work his culinary magic on stage. From there, he took the show to venues across Australia and New Zealand.

In November 2000, a slightly edited version of *The Naked Chef* television show premiered on the Food Network in the United States. The show aired on Saturday nights at 9:30 P.M. To promote the show, Oliver appeared on numerous American talk shows to discuss his recipes and philosophical approach to cooking, and even to demonstrate his skills. During one stop, for example, he cooked homemade pasta with *Today* hosts Matt Lauer and Katie Couric. His show became an instant hit in the United States and many other countries. By 2001 *The Naked Chef* was airing on sixty-four channels in thirty-four different countries, including Australia, South Africa, Italy, France, and Germany. Millions of people around the world watched him cook every week.

As with British critics, reviewers in the United States were mixed regarding the show's style, despite the fact that audiences seemed to love it. Often the same reviewer had both positive and negative things to say about Oliver. For example, one reviewer loved that "this gravy-boat dreamboat is professional and informative," but also complained that "his languid preening, the jerky handheld camera and the Brit-pop sound track are enough to make you want to toss your biscotti."[55] Oliver did not put much stock in reviews, though. "If the Press realised the stick [flak] that I have to put up with when I'm explaining the passion I feel about England and our food and our chefs, I think they'd shut up,"[56] he says.

Sexiest Chef Alive

Oliver's blue eyes, tousled blond hair, and impish grin made him a big hit with women around the world—and at home. After *The Naked Chef* became a hit, his younger sister, Anna-Marie, commented, "Suddenly, I have a lot of women friends asking if they can come 'round when we have a family barbecue."[57] In 2000, *People* magazine named Oliver the "sexiest chef" in its annual "Sexiest Men Alive" issue.

Oliver had no idea what all the fuss was about. "I think I am pretty average, boring looking, really,"[58] he said. Oliver has never considered himself a sex symbol or a style icon. He has always felt more comfortable in a sweatshirt and jeans or old clothes bought from a secondhand store than in a suit and tie. Also, Oliver has never been very smooth with women. Instead, he uses food to win their hearts. "If you really want to get your missus going, do something delicate, like a bit of fish stuffed with herbs, olive oil and white wine," he once

Not as Easy as It Looks

In his show, *The Naked Chef,* Jamie Oliver showed British and American audiences how easy it was for him to whip up a delicious Italian meal. In his cookbook of the same name, he wrote how easy it would be for his readers to cook the same food. "The aim of this book is to inspire you to get into the kitchen, fired with enthusiasm and confidence," [1] Oliver writes.

Yet many people who have read *The Naked Chef*—and its sequels—are not convinced that Oliver's recipes are as easy to make as they look. "Making your own pasta is not 'quicker than walking down to the supermarket,'"[2] a reviewer from *People* magazine complains. American readers who have posted comments about the book online say some ingredients are hard to find in the United States, and they disagree with Oliver's claim that anyone can cook homemade pasta on a weeknight. Overall, though, reviewers love his hip approach to cookbook writing. "This is functional home cooking at its grooviest," writes *Publishers Weekly.* "Oliver delivers a hip classic that will appeal to a new generation of modern epicureans who face the challenge of cooking within the confines of tiny urban kitchens on time-pressed schedules."[3]

1. Jamie Oliver. *The Naked Chef.* New York: Hyperion, 2000.
2. James Oliver. "Picks and Pans Review: *The Naked Chef.*" *People,* October 2, 2000. www.people.com/people/archive/article/0,,20132442,00.html.
3. *Publishers Weekly.* "*The Naked Chef,*" October 9, 2000. www.publishersweekly.com/978-0-7868-6617-5.

said. "Bake it in tinfoil. You break that open and the smells go everywhere. And then you say, 'This is what I made for you.' Girls like that."[59] Although his girlfriend, Jools, loves Oliver's looks and his cooking, she thinks he is far too down to earth to be considered one of the "sexiest men alive." "You'd never know he was supposed to be a sex symbol," she says. "He's not vain at all."[60]

Oliver might have broken a lot of hearts when he proposed to Jools on Christmas Eve, 1999. He asked her to marry him while she was placing a wreath on her father's grave. (Her father died in 1997 after suffering a stroke.) "His way, I think, of asking my dad's permission to marry me,"[61] she says.

On June 24, 2000, the couple was married at All Saints Church in Rickling Green, Essex, just down the road from Oliver's parents' house. (He walked from their home to the church

Oliver and girlfriend Juliette Norton wed on June 24, 2000. The couple was married at All Saints Church in Rickling Green, Essex, just down the road from Oliver's parents' house.

for the wedding.) The bride wore a strapless white satin wedding gown. Oliver, in his unconventional style, wore a baby-blue corduroy suit with a pink shirt and purple socks.

An Elvis impersonator sang "Can't Help Falling in Love" for the one hundred guests who gathered in the thirteenth-century church. As Oliver waited for his bride (she was a few minutes late), he commented, "It's more nerve-racking than cooking for Tony Blair." Oliver's father, Trevor, walked Jools down the aisle. After the wedding, Oliver said of marrying his sweetheart, "It was beautiful. I'm bloody happy."[62]

Oliver credits his down-to-earth wife with keeping him grounded during his meteoric rise to fame. "Jools is interesting cos she's not like me at all," Oliver says. "She hasn't got a mission, she just wants to be married to someone she loves and have a family and that's it, end of story."[63]

Saying Good-bye to *The Naked Chef*

While his wife stayed grounded, however, Oliver's ambition kept growing. By the third season of *The Naked Chef*, he was a huge star. In 2001 he decided it was time to move beyond the production company that had launched his career and start his own production company. This was not good news to the show's producer, Patricia Llewellyn, who felt as though she were being abandoned by the TV personality she had created.

It also was not good news for her production company, which was relying on the show's big earnings. "It was awful for the company," admits Llewellyn. "He's a born entrepreneur, he wanted his own production company, and it was normal that he'd do it but I learned a business lesson—not to put all your eggs in one basket." However, she was resigned to Oliver's moving on. "Perhaps it's the first agent syndrome. You dump the person who discovered you,"[64] she adds.

One chapter of Oliver's life had ended. It was a short but highly successful chapter, especially for someone still only in his mid-twenties. Although *The Naked Chef* was now behind him, there were more shows to produce and more food-related ventures to launch, including Oliver's first big charity project.

Chapter 4

A Culinary Star with a Good Heart

Just a couple of years after *The Naked Chef* premiered on British television, Jamie Oliver was an international success. Yet inside, he was still just a simple boy from a small English town. "I am a village boy at heart," he says. "I want to live in a little village on the outskirts of Cambridge and have my own [restaurant], with Jools doing the front of the house [working upfront]. I can't wait."[65] Oliver's dream of owning a small country restaurant and having Jools serve as manager/hostess would have to wait, however; plans for a very different kind of restaurant were about to move ahead.

Fifteen

As far back as 1995, Oliver had had the desire to help kids who had dropped out of school or lost their way in life. He felt a kinship with these wayward kids, having dropped out of traditional school himself at age sixteen. In 2002, with the money and fame he had earned from his television shows and books, Oliver decided to make his dream a reality. He came up with the idea for a restaurant called Fifteen. The concept was to teach disadvantaged young people how to run a world-class restaurant and, by doing so, set them up for a more productive future. "A lot of my students, like me, were never particularly suited to school," he explains. "And the lovely thing about cooking is you don't have to be able to do economics or maths or spelling to do well."[66]

Every year, Fifteen hires fifteen young people aged eighteen to twenty-four. Those selected are referred to the program by British government agencies such as the prison service and by private organizations that help youths in trouble. "Most of these kids have terrible family situations, and when we've been able to replace those with the Fifteen family and keep the positive messages coming, then the kids are more likely to succeed in the long term—versus slipping back into their old habits,"[67] Oliver says.

The students who enroll in Fifteen take classes and do a one-year apprenticeship with professional chefs in the restaurant's kitchen. They earn £100 ($155) per week, plus a £30-per-week ($47) bonus if they show up for all their shifts. Fifteen is not an easy program. Each year up to six apprentices may drop out. But those who make it through the program learn not just how to cook and run a restaurant, but also how to manage their money in the real world.

Each year, fifteen disadvantaged people ranging in ages from eighteen to twenty-four are selected to apprentice at one of Oliver's Fifteen restaurants. The students not only learn to cook and run a business but to manage their money as well.

The program meant so much to Oliver that he invested $640,000 of his own money to get the project started. He also takes no profit from it: All of the proceeds Fifteen earns are put right back into the restaurant to help future groups of students. "I'm pretty nice most of the time but sometimes Jamie still makes me look bad because he's got such a big heart,"[68] says Tony Elvin, Fifteen's training and development manager.

Fifteen's training process was filmed for a program that aired on Channel 4 in Britain called *Jamie's Kitchen*. More than five million people watched the 2002 series. As with many of Oliver's projects, Fifteen also spawned a tie-in book of the same name.

Despite being staffed by young chefs, Fifteen has won its share of awards. In 2003 the upscale *Tatler* magazine gave Fifteen its best-restaurant award. The Tio Pepe Carlton London Restaurant Awards also presented Fifteen with its Academy Award of Excellence. Fifteen was not a hit with everyone—some patrons complained about the "careless" service and "extraordinarily overpriced"[69] meals. Critics, however, raved about the food. "From first to last, it was exceptional,"[70] wrote a reviewer from the *Guardian*. Just a year after opening, Fifteen was getting two thousand requests a day for tables.

Fifteen was so successful that Oliver decided to expand the enterprise. In 2004 he opened the first Fifteen franchise in Amsterdam, Netherlands. That was followed in 2006 by a franchise in Melbourne, Australia, and another in southwestern England's coastal tourist area of Cornwall. Oliver's mark is all over these restaurants. "There's no escaping him here, his spirit pervades the place: zingy Italian-inspired food; disarmingly friendly staff; chatty menus peppered with 'amazings' and 'fantastics,'"[71] wrote the *Guardian*'s Jon Henley in 2012. Along one wall of the Cornwall Fifteen's dining room is scrawled Oliver's signature in bright pink.

While training young chefs, these restaurants have also been financially successful. The Cornwall Fifteen serves about eighty thousand customers annually, bringing in more than £3 million ($4.6 million).

Graduating Fifteen

Fifteen was more than just a side project or another hit TV series for Jamie Oliver. The celebrity chef created it not to make money or earn big ratings but to help young people who needed a hand. "Fifteen is not some airy-fairy TV show. It's for life,"[1] Oliver says. "They come to us ex-prison, ex-drugs, homeless and directionless, and blossom and go off to work in some of the world's best restaurants. It's remarkable."[2]

Fifteen provides troubled kids with a lifetime's worth of training. Kids who participate learn how to season food, how to turn olives into olive oil, and how free-range living can affect an animal's taste and texture. Graduates of the program have said Fifteen truly changed their lives. "I don't know what I'd be doing if it hadn't been for this. Working in a cardboard box factory, probably,"[3] says Emily Hunt, who was part of the sixth graduating class of the Cornwall Fifteen restaurant.

1. Quoted in Jessica Gunn. "Passing On the Passion." *Caterer & Hotelkeeper*, November 27, 2003, p. 22.
2. Quoted in *Cosmopolitan*. "Fun Fearless Male: Jamie Oliver," December 2006.
3. Jon Henley. "Jamie Oliver's Fifteen: A Winning Recipe." *Guardian* (Manchester, UK), April 9, 2012. www.guardian.co.uk/society/2012/apr/09/jamie-oliver-fifteen-winning-recipe.

Dishing Up a Profit

Its profitability notwithstanding, Fifteen was meant to be a charitable venture, but Oliver also created a line of restaurants that were intended to make a profit. In 2008 he launched a chain of casual Italian restaurants called Jamie's Italian. The chain's first restaurant opened in Oxford, with a menu filled with Oliver's takes on Italian dishes such as wild truffle risotto and grilled free-range chicken.

One reviewer for the *Guardian* raved about the taste of the food: "Particularly splendid was a bruschetta with crispy pancetta [Italian-style bacon]," he wrote. "Also great were three pasta dishes, penne arrabiata zinging with hot chilies, 'lovely and sweet' linguine with prawns, and a richly satisfying pappardelle with sausage."[72] The reviewer's "negatives" included the nearly forty-minute wait outside (the restaurant does not accept reservations) and its less-than-authentic approach to Italian cuisine. By 2013 Oliver had opened more than fifteen Jamie's Italian restaurants all over England, as well as in Dubai, United Arab Emirates. He was also looking to open up two franchises in Russia.

Oliver also launched two other restaurant ventures. One was called Union Jacks, which specializes in a British version of wood-fire cooking and flatbread pizzas. This chain was a collaborative effort between Oliver and American chef Chris Bianco, whom Oliver called a "fellow food 'geek.'"[73] As of 2013, there were four Union Jacks around the London area. His other

Jamie's Italian was created as a chain restaurant with a casual atmosphere that served up Oliver's take on a variety of Italian dishes. By 2013 Oliver had opened more than fifteen Jamie's Italian locations all over the world.

restaurant, Barbecoa, was created with another American chef, Adam Perry Lang. Located in the heart of London, Barbecoa is an American-style barbecue and steakhouse.

Having so many restaurants operating simultaneously can make it hard for a chef to be very hands-on, which might account for the poor reviews some of these ventures received. Jay Rayner, a reviewer at the *Guardian*, while praising the two offerings of ribs on the menu, found nothing else on the menu any good and called Barbecoa "underwhelming. . . . If this restaurant opened in New York, its shortcomings would see it laughed out of town."[74]

Despite such complaints, Oliver's food was getting a reputation for being approachable and down-to-earth. It was not the fancy cuisine on which many of his fellow celebrity chefs had built their reputations. Oliver is happiest when he creates food that reaches the masses, as he was raised to do in his parents' pub. "I'd like to win a Michelin star but it's unlikely," he admits. "My cooking just ain't fiddly [fussy] enough and that's fine by me. Half of those 100 pound a head places aren't half as good as the stuff my old Dad serves up by the fire with a pint of Guinness for 8 pounds."[75]

Jamie Escapes

While cultivating his restaurants, Oliver still nurtured his television and book projects. In 2005, just before his thirtieth birthday, Oliver took off for Italy to film a series called *Jamie's Great Italian Escape*. In the program, Oliver drives around the country in a restored 1956 camper van, complete with a kitchen trailer. His goal with the show was to cook with some of the greatest Italian chefs and rediscover what originally made him fall in love with Italian cooking. He also wanted to prove that English cooking was far better than people in other European countries believed.

As usual, the TV series had a companion book. This one was called *Jamie's Italy*. The book went to number one on the bestseller list in Great Britain. It sold more copies during the week before Christmas than any other nonfiction book had done before it, and it was nominated for the British Book Award's "Book of the Year."

While his TV shows earned massive ratings, his books sold out of bookstores, and his restaurants overflowed with satisfied customers, Oliver looked at other markets in which he could showcase his growing brand. In addition to serving as the face of Sainsbury's supermarkets, Oliver launched his own line of dishes, cookware, gift foods, and Italian foods. He developed a product called the Flavour Shaker, which grinds and mixes herbs for cooking. People around the world can buy cast-iron cookware, blenders, glasses, plates, seasonings, and even cheeses and meats that all bear the Jamie Oliver brand. They can even sell the products themselves, through Jamie at Home—his line of cooking products that is sold via at-home parties.

Oliver also opened a cooking shop, called Recipease, in the Notting Hill Gate section of London. Two more locations followed, in the town of Brighton (along the southern England coast) and Clapham Junction (in central London). Visitors to the store can take a one-hour cooking lesson for about £40 ($62), in which they learn how to make a fragrant Thai green curry or stuffed homemade pasta. Those who are not interested in cooking for themselves can pick up a prepared meal to go, or eat in the shop's café.

Proceeds from his TV shows, restaurants, endorsements, and products added up. By 2012, Oliver was worth an estimated £150 million ($234 million). He was far wealthier than many of his celebrity chef contemporaries, such as Bobby Flay (worth an estimated $6 million in 2012, according to Complex.com), Paula Deen ($16 million), and Rachel Ray ($60 to $100 million). One of the few celebrity chefs who outearned Oliver was iconic chef/restaurateur Wolfgang Puck (worth an estimated $400 million).

Making Time for Family

As important as a successful career was to Oliver, family still came first. On March 18, 2002, Oliver and Jools welcomed their

Oliver opened a cooking shop called Recipease that features cooking classes and meals to go, as well as utensils, books, and grocery items.

first child, a girl named Poppy Honey Rosie Oliver. Daisy Boo Pamela was born a year later, on April 10, 2003. Another sister, Petal Blossom Rainbow, came along on April 3, 2009. Being surrounded by females was a little overwhelming for Oliver. "I love my girls but as a man they baffle me," he says. On September

Unique Baby Names

Jamie Oliver and his wife, Jools, got pretty creative when it came to choosing their children's names—Poppy Honey Rosie, Petal Blossom Rainbow, Daisy Boo Pamela, and Buddy Bear Maurice. Jools says she gave each of her children three names because she could not decide on just one or two. Maurice was a tribute to Jools's father, who died in 1997, but she chose many of the other names just because she liked them. (Petal Rainbow is the name of a My Little Pony doll, for example.)

The Olivers are not the only celebrity couple to raise eyebrows with their odd choice of children's names. Actress Gwyneth Paltrow and her husband, Coldplay lead singer Chris Martin, named their daughter Apple when she was born in 2004. Magician Penn Jillette and his wife, Emily, named their daughter Moxie CrimeFighter and their son Zolten Penn. Perhaps most famously, pop icon Michael Jackson named both of his sons Prince Michael but referred to one of them as "Blanket."

15, 2010, Jools finally gave birth to a son, whom she and Oliver named Buddy Bear Maurice. "Buddy is fantastic, a proper little boy—cute as pie and loves his Dad,"[76] Oliver beams.

Up until then, the couple had lived in a home Oliver owned in the Hampstead section of London. Oliver eventually sold the Hampstead home and moved his family into a £3-million ($4.7 million) home in London's exclusive Primrose Hill section. When the house next door went up for sale in 2009, Oliver bought it for £3.5 million ($5.5 million) and combined the two properties into a nineteen-room mansion, complete with a state-of the-art, $300,000 chef's kitchen. The new house also featured a large reception area and his-and-her dressing rooms on the first floor. Both houses were painted canary yellow, and the balconies on the first floors were redesigned to match one another and form one unified home.

Whereas money was no issue for the celebrity chef, finding family time was challenging. Oliver worked twelve-hour days while his wife stayed home and cared for the children. "Maybe one evening every two weeks Jamie comes home and we eat together," says Jools. "I'm used to it now and it's fine."[77] While

The Oliver family has grown by four since the marriage of Jools and Jamie. Daughter Poppy was born in 2002, followed by two more girls in 2003 and 2009 and finally a son in 2010.

filming his shows or tending to his restaurants, Oliver often has to be away from his wife and children for long stretches of time. "At times like these I really miss Jools and the kids," he said during the filming of one of his television shows on Italy's Amalfi Coast. "I want to be a brilliant dad, and I think I am a good dad. But I think also the other half of my life is my job."[78]

Oliver makes weekends his refuge from work—time to spend with his wife and children. The family often escapes to their other home—a country estate in Essex, just down a few winding country roads from the pub run by his parents. "The weekends are ours and I just look forward to them," says Jools. "Jamie is religious about keeping the weekends for us, for being a dad,"[79] she adds. On the weekends Oliver also tries to find time to catch up on a few of his favorite hobbies, which include fishing and running.

Yet even at his vacation home, his work life sometimes intrudes. In 2006, for example, Oliver filmed a Channel 4 series called *Jamie at Home* at his Essex estate. Using fruits and vegetables grown in his own garden and cooking in his own kitchens (the house has four of them and a wood-fired oven outside), Oliver set out to prove once again that home-cooked food made with basic, simple ingredients is best.

Jamie and Jools's marriage has not always been easy, given the demands of Oliver's career and the attention he has received from fans, particularly women. Yet they have found a place where both of them can be happy. "Jamie and I trust each other, even though we are apart a lot and he works with a load of women," says Jools. "I used to mind. Ten years ago things were really difficult, but now I trust him—I am very secure."[80] "We love each other to bits,"[81] says Oliver.

The challenges to his personal life would continue, however, as Oliver prepared to launch one of his most ambitious ventures yet. This time, he was not just cooking or opening a restaurant. He was trying to save lives.

Chapter 5

Food Revolution

Food has always been an important part of Oliver's life—from his childhood at his parent's pub to the cooking shows that made him famous. Yet he realized early on that food, while delicious and wonderful to eat, can also be dangerous, especially when people eat too much of the wrong foods. Obesity—having an unhealthy amount of body fat—is a serious health risk. People who are obese are more likely to get cancer or heart disease and die young. Obesity is a big problem in England, which is considered the fattest nation in Europe. According to the British government, nearly two-thirds of the British population is overweight or obese.

Oliver became very concerned that his fellow Britons were overindulging in unhealthy foods such as french fries and burgers. For his next project he wanted to try to improve the quality of the English diet. He thought it made sense to start where bad eating habits begin—in childhood.

Jamie's School Dinners

To champion healthful eating, in 2005 Oliver targeted the place where children spend most of their days and eat many of their meals—in school. Many of the school lunches (the English call them "school dinners") in Great Britain were notoriously unhealthy—high in fat, sugar, and salt and low in nutritional content—and Oliver wanted to change that. "A school meal accounts for one-third of a child's daily nutritional intake," he says. "For many children up and down the country, the majority of food they are fed at home is either made up of ready meals,

Kidbrooke Comprehensive secondary school in southeast London received a lunch menu overhaul by Oliver. The kitchen staff changed their style of cooking and began serving healthier fare.

takeaways [food taken out from quick-service restaurants] or—in the worst cases—nothing at all. This means the meal they eat at school will be the only nutritious food they eat that day. Encouraging children to make better food choices at school is absolutely vital."[82]

The school he targeted for improvement was Kidbrooke Comprehensive, a secondary school (for children aged eleven to eighteen) in the Greenwich section of southeast London. The process of overhauling the school lunch program was filmed for a four-part television series called *Jamie's School Dinners*, which premiered in February 2005. At first, the Kidbrooke school administration was hesitant to let Oliver spotlight the poor quality of its lunch program. "I had reservations about letting the cameras into school because I was aware of the danger of showing up aspects of school life you would rather keep within these walls," says Kidbrooke's headteacher (principal), Trisha Jaffe, "but overall, the benefits outweighed any disadvantages because it was hard to pass up getting involved with someone who had the influence to shake things up and to cut through any red tape."[83]

When Oliver got to Kidbrooke, he discovered that the seven hundred students were lunching on a daily diet of burgers, french fries, pizza, soda, and strips of processed meat known as Turkey Twizzlers. Their diet at home did not seem to be much better, either. "Early on I took a whole load of vegetables into a class and most kids were hard pushed to identify them," Oliver says. "They'd never seen a leek, let alone eaten one."[84]

So he set out to change the menu. Oliver introduced more fruits and vegetables into the lunch offerings and took away the unhealthy french fries and burgers. It was not easy getting kids who were so used to eating junk food to accept nutritious alternatives. Oliver had to be a bit sneaky, especially with the vegetables. "You'd hide them in the pizza topping, or pulp them into a vegetable stock so that the kids got the goodness without realising it,"[85] he says.

Oliver rejects the idea that the only thing kids will eat is junk food. "It takes some effort to get them to try new things, and they may not like *everything*, but there will always be some vegetable or dish that the kids will eat,"[86] he says. To demonstrate to the students how important it is to eat healthfully and keep their weight under control, Oliver put on a "fat suit" (a garment that gives the wearer the appearance of being obese) and his scooter appeared to almost collapse under his increased weight.

A Campaign for Better Eating

In *Jamie's School Dinners*, Oliver reveals another surprising fact about school meals in England. Each lunch costs only 37p (pence) (57¢) to make—a quarter of the cost of the average prison dinner in England. Oliver thought this was not nearly enough to spend on each child's lunch. He knew that schools needed more money if they were going to serve more-healthful meals, and the place to get that extra money was from the British government.

To this end, Oliver launched a national campaign called Feed Me Better, with the aim of encouraging the British government to spend more on improving the quality of the country's school lunches. He promised that the investment would be well worth the cost. "If changes are made it will only be a matter of months before British health, education and farming could be affected for the better," he said. "It could be one of the biggest food revolutions that England has ever seen."[87] Oliver was so determined to fight for better nutrition that one reviewer called his campaign a "jihad [holy war] against junk food."[88]

To convince the British government to get on his side, Oliver created an online petition, which he filled with more than 270,000 signatures. Both parents and politicians got involved. On March 30, 2005, the petition made its way to 10 Downing Street, the residence of then–prime minister Tony Blair. Oliver got the prime minister's attention. Blair pledged £280 million ($435 million) to provide Britain's schools with improved cooking facilities, training for dinner ladies (the name for school cafeteria staff in England), and better-quality food. He also set up a School Meals Review Panel to investigate the country's school lunch program. "It may take a little time to change children's tastes but it will be worth the effort if we can get them enjoying healthy and good quality food at school,"[89] said Blair.

In 2006 British education secretary Alan Johnson announced that schools would replace unhealthy foods such as burgers, potato chips, sodas, and chocolate candy with more freshly cooked meals, fruits, and vegetables. The government increased the money spent on each school lunch from 37p (57¢) to between 50 and 60p (77¢ to 93¢). In September 2007, the government pledged another £240 million ($372 million) to make school lunches more affordable for students. The government also set up a School Food Trust to help schools establish better nutritional standards.

For Oliver's efforts, in 2006 England's Channel 4 television network awarded him its "most inspiring political figure of the year" award. Yet his goal was not to make a political statement. Oliver says he just wants to change and save lives. "At heart, I'm probably no more political than anyone else," he says. "But because of what I do, people listen to me."[90] He also insists that

Eat to Save Your Life

Jamie Oliver was on a mission to help the people of England eat better-quality, more-healthful foods. After he helped revolutionize school meals with *Jamie's School Dinners*, Oliver moved on to launch several other healthful-eating initiatives that aired as television specials or series.

Eat to Save Your Life (2008) focused on eighteen overweight Britons. Oliver, along with a team of doctors, nutritionists, and fitness experts, showed how these people's diets were putting them at risk for cancer and other serious diseases. The show also featured a very graphic autopsy, in which a doctor cut open and examined the insides of a 350-pound man (159kg) who had essentially eaten himself to death.

Jamie's Fowl Dinners also aired in 2008. This show pointed the spotlight on Britain's poultry industry. In the show, Oliver killed, butchered, cooked, and served chickens to a live audience to illustrate the appalling conditions under which some chickens are raised and killed. After the show aired, sales of free-range and organic poultry jumped by 50 percent in England.

That same year, another show, *Jamie's Ministry of Food,* showed Oliver setting up an instructional center in Rotherham (a town in northern England, near Sheffield) to teach the townspeople how to cook more healthfully using fresh ingredients. The center was replicated in other English towns. Today there are six Ministry of Food locations throughout England, and the program has expanded to Australia, too.

In 2009 the show *Jamie Saves Our Bacon* revealed the appalling conditions in England's pig farming industry. Like many of Oliver's other such specials, it was disgusting to watch at certain points.

he is not out to earn ratings or make money with his campaign against unhealthy school meals. He says that this is more than just a program—he is determined to fundamentally change the way people view and consume food. "It's a campaign, rather than a TV series," he says. "We've got to make a difference."[91]

Benefits . . . and Backlash

Oliver's campaign gained ground quickly, but it was not without snags. For one, he was asking for a major transformation in a very short period of time. "Jamie Oliver kick-started a welcomed revolution which brought about a much-needed injection of Government cash," explains Beverley Baker, former chairman of the Local Authority Caterers Association (LACA)—the organization that represents companies that provide school meals in England. "But we were then catapulted into trying to 'undo' 20 years of neglect and under-funding as well as a culture fixed on fast food,"[92] Baker adds.

One of the biggest challenges Oliver faced in transforming England's school lunch program was that the people who cooked the meals had little training in healthful meal preparation or actual cooking. In the past, dinner ladies just heated up prepared foods. For the first time, they would have to prepare meals themselves. "Overnight, we were expected to start seasoning meat and peeling hundreds of carrots—but that takes time and we're not being paid for it," says Cathy Stewart, a dinner lady in Hackney, London. Many of England's dinner ladies made less than £5 ($7.75) an hour. "They want dinner ladies to become professional chefs. But they won't give us the resources we need,"[93] she adds.

It was also not easy to transform children's diets overnight, especially when the students were so used to eating junk food. Some parents complained about the taste—and high price (the equivalent of nearly four dollars per lunch)—of Oliver's new school menus. Instead of encouraging their kids to buy the more healthful school lunches, they supplied them with fish and chips, burgers, and fries. In other cases, parents packed their children's lunches full of chocolate and potato chips—foods that Oliver had fought so hard to get out of the schools. "We just want to make sure the kids are properly fed," one parent told the *Daily Mirror* newspaper. "They don't enjoy the school food and the end result is that they're starving."[94]

In fact, there was so much resistance to Oliver's efforts that after he introduced his changes to school menus, the number of children who bought school lunches in England dropped by 15 to 20 percent. A year into the program, one journalist asked, "Are school canteens [lunch rooms] happier and healthier places? Hardly. Dinner ladies are threatening to strike; catering companies are worried about going bust; and parents are opting for unhealthier packed lunches. Thanks, Jamie."[95]

Despite such criticisms and push-back, the backlash seemed temporary. Just a couple of years later, school lunches in England had undergone major improvements. There were fewer french fries and pizzas and more fruits, vegetables, pasta, and fish on the menus. Eventually the kids got on board with more-healthful eating, and more of them started to buy school lunches again. Interestingly, once they began to eat better, the students' academic performance improved. Test scores were up by nearly 5 percent, according to a study conducted by researchers at Oxford and Essex Universities. "I think things are going well," said

Although healthier meals were being served at school, there was a decline in the number of students buying lunch after revisions to the menu. A few years later, students got on board with healthier eating and showed improvement on test scores.

Oliver in 2010. "We always thought it would take 10 years to really see a difference but there are already figures that show up-take is increasing and that kids eating a healthy lunch program perform better at school."[96]

"It's About Setting Kids Up for Life"

To show just how committed he was to the success of his healthier schools project, Oliver promised to give a percentage of the future profits from each of his companies to continue to improve meals and food education in Britain's schools. Giving

In 2011 Oliver launched another healthy school program called Jamie's Kitchen Garden Project, which helps English schoolchildren plant their own gardens and cook the food they grow.

back was important to Oliver. He had earned millions of pounds doing what he loved and wanted to share it. By 2010 he had given £2.7 million ($4 million) to charity and ranked number twenty-two on the *Sunday Times*'s Giving List.

To continue in the spirit of giving, in 2011 Oliver launched another healthy school program called Jamie's Kitchen Garden Project, which helps English schoolchildren plant their own gardens and cook the food they grow. "Kids love growing stuff," Oliver says. "And when they grow fruits and vegetables, they are really happy to eat fruits and vegetables,"[97] he adds. The program was piloted at Orford Primary School in Suffolk, near the eastern coast of England. There, the kids planted fresh vegetables (such as brussels sprouts, tomatoes, and peas), fruits (like apples and strawberries), and herbs, which they used to cook homemade dishes like crispy rosemary potatoes and vegetable frittatas. They even created their own recipe for pasta sauce, which they bottled and sold in their community. A second garden program was launched at Rotherfield Primary School in the Islington section of London. Oliver's goal was to eventually roll out the Kitchen Garden Project in other schools as well. "It's about setting kids up for life,"[98] says Oliver. "We want to get gardens in every school in the country. . . . We're passionate about teaching kids to grow, where food comes from and how it affects our bodies."[99]

In England, Oliver's school initiative seemed to be a success. Yet he could not be sure that he would have the same luck when he took his ideas across the Atlantic Ocean to the United States.

Coming to America

Like a food missionary, Oliver next wanted to spread his message of healthful eating across the globe. He felt that the United States was an important place to get his message across. As in his home nation, Americans struggle with obesity and being overweight: The Centers for Disease Control and Prevention (CDC) reports that more than one-third of Americans are obese and that another one-third are overweight. Oliver had enjoyed success in changing Britain's school meals program and getting English people to eat more healthfully, and he wanted to attempt the same thing in the States. So in 2009, he temporarily left his wife (who was pregnant with their fourth child) and family to travel nearly 4,000 miles (6,437km) to the United States. He filmed his journey for the ABC television series *Jamie Oliver's Food Revolution*.

Oliver focused his efforts on Huntington, West Virginia—a town that at the time had the highest obesity rate in the country, according to the CDC. Half of the adults who lived there were obese. Oliver's goal was to expose the poor eating habits in both the town's homes and schools. What he did not anticipate was how badly the people of Huntington would react to his attempt to change their diet. "You can imagine how eagerly the people of West Virginia respond to a foreigner with meticulously rumpled hair and a funny accent telling them to hand over the fries,"[100] a *Washington Post* reporter sarcastically wrote. Oliver was met with resistance almost immediately. When he was interviewed at the local country radio station, for example, the interviewer grumbled at him, "We don't want to sit around and eat lettuce all day. Who made you king?"[101]

Oliver brought his passion for healthy eating to the United States, where one-third of all Americans are obese and one-third are overweight.

Yet Oliver did not give up. For six weeks, he worked with local officials, parents, and schools to improve the town's eating habits. At Central City Elementary School, Oliver watched in horror as lunch ladies Paulie, Millie, Linda, Louella, and Alice prepared breakfast pizza topped with eggs, sausage, and cheese and served it with a side of sugary flavored milk. He helped them revise the school's menu and taught them healthful cooking skills, such as how to marinate fresh chicken breasts and make their own homemade salad dressings.

Oliver also visited local families, including the Edwards family. He confronted the mother, Stacie, about the unhealthy junk food she had been feeding her kids. He piled all of the fatty, greasy foods—such as donuts, pizza, and french fries—that she had fed her kids in the past week into the middle of the kitchen table. "This is going to kill your children early," he told her. "We're talking about 10, 13, 14 years off their life."[102] Stacie was reduced to tears.

When it aired in March 2010, *Jamie Oliver's Food Revolution* was a ratings and critical success. It attracted 7.5 million viewers and won an Emmy Award for Best Reality Series. That same month, Oliver received the TED (Technology, Entertainment, Design) Award, which is given to people who change the world through innovation.

Yet when it came to achieving its aim of improving Americans' eating habits, *Jamie Oliver's Food Revolution* was a failure. "The reality behind 'Food Revolution' is that after the first two months of the new meals, children were overwhelmingly unhappy with the food, milk consumption plummeted and many students dropped out of the school lunch program,"[103] wrote one reviewer. Oliver's changes also sent school food costs soaring. And despite being more healthful in some ways, his meals did not meet the state's nutritional standards for school lunches. Ironically, most of them contained more total fat or more saturated fat, and almost half had fewer calories than the West Virginia Board of Education requires for school lunches. This left Huntington school officials fearing that they would lose federal funding for their school lunch program.

Food Revolution—Take Two

The second season of *Jamie Oliver's Food Revolution*, filmed in 2011, was not any more successful. In fact, it had problems from the very start. This time, Oliver tried to introduce more fresh foods into Southern California's Los Angeles Unified School District (LAUSD)—the second-largest school district in the country. But LAUSD superintendent Ramon Cortines was not interested. He withdrew Oliver's permit to film in the district's schools and accused the TV host of making the school district into a "stage." Oliver was even kicked off the local high school campus when he tried to film there. Oliver responded by stating in the *Los Angeles Times*, "Ramon Cortines, you should be ashamed of yourself."[104]

Barred from the city's schools, he turned his attention to other areas. Oliver met with local children and their parents. He distributed free healthful lunches (featuring guacamole and smoked turkey wraps, milk, and fresh fruit) outside a Los Angeles public school. He tried to encourage one Los Angeles–area fast food restaurant to take french fries off of its menu (he was unsuccessful). Oliver even walked around the Los Angeles streets dressed up one time as a giant peapod and another time as a tomato to get his message across.

Despite being banned from Los Angeles schools, Oliver still had an impact there. He sent out a petition, which collected thousands of signatures, and launched a letter-writing campaign, trying to push for changes in the school district's lunch program. When a new LAUSD superintendent, Dr. John Deasy, took over in April 2011, he was much more receptive to the idea of healthful food in the district's schools. That month, the LAUSD announced that it would introduce a revamped menu the following fall. Junk foods and flavored milk were removed from the menu, while more-healthful items such as Indian chicken tandoori, pad Thai noodles, vegetable curries, and quinoa (a South American grain) salads were added.

It was a temporary victory, however. Six months after the new menu debuted, hundreds of high school students refused to eat the new meals. "Things were positive at the start but now kids

Jamie Oliver and the Pink Slime

In 2011 a new phrase entered the American vocabulary: pink slime. The name referred to Lean Finely Textured Beef (LFTB), a pink-colored gooey substance made when scraps of beef are heated, put in a machine to separate out the fat, and then treated with the chemical ammonium hydroxide.

Oliver brought the issue of pink slime to light in an April 2011 episode of his show *Food Revolution*. In March 2012 ABC News and other U.S. news organizations broke the story that pink slime was being served at McDonald's and sold at many supermarket chains. Millions of Americans were disgusted and outraged. The furor led many stores and restaurants to stop carrying the product. In May 2012, Beef Products Inc., the South Dakota–based company that produces LFTB, was forced to shut down its three factories. The company, and one of its employees who had been fired over the issue, filed a lawsuit against Oliver and the other news organizations that had started the backlash against its product.

Pictured here is the ammonia-treated filler made from beef scraps, also known as "pink slime."

have made it clear to us, 'This is not what we want,'" said Anna Redd, a teacher at West Adams Preparatory High School. "It is so sad to see, because now we have trash cans full of tomatoes, lettuce, broccoli and other vegetables."[105]

When Los Angeles schools put pizza back on the menu, Oliver was furious. "It's decisions like that that [make] me crazy," he says. "It's absolutely the government's responsibility to feed children properly at school, 180 days a year. *Properly* means fresh food, cooked from scratch by someone who cares. It's not rocket science; it just takes training for the cooks and education for the kids."[106] Despite his efforts to promote more-healthful eating, Oliver was criticized for failing to understand the American diet and Americans' cultural relationship with food. "He will fail, of course, not for lack of effort but because he just doesn't get the fact that excessive consumption is woven into our national DNA,"[107] wrote *Esquire* columnist Stephen Marche.

Trying to Change the World One Meal at a Time

Despite the setbacks with all of his school food initiatives, Oliver believes that he has at least achieved victory by initiating a conversation about healthful eating. As he puts it, "We've started a national dialog around food issues that many more people in America are participating in part because of exposure to our shows and campaigns."[108] And he refuses to give up. In 2011, for example, Oliver made his plea for more-healthful eating to heads of state and United Nations members from across the world at a disease summit in New York. He called for a "global movement to make obesity a human rights issue."[109]

On May 19, 2012, Oliver launched the first annual global Food Revolution Day, which was created to educate people around the world about healthful food. The day was marked by more than a thousand events—from cooking classes to community potluck suppers. "I can not tell you how proud I am that we have more than 500 cities in 57 countries around the world

GET INVOLVED ON

FOOD REVOLUTION ★ DAY ★

a global day of action aimed to inspire people to get cooking and champion better food skills for people of all ages.

COOK IT. SHARE IT. LIVE IT

17th May 2013

Find out more at www.foodrevolutionday.com

Food Revolution Day is a campaign of Jamie Oliver's charities: the Better Food Foundation (UK) and Jamie Oliver Food Foundation (USA), and our partners at The Good Foundation (AUS).

The first annual global Food Revolution Day was created to educate people around the world about healthful food.

standing up for real food,"[110] he says. Even his critics admired his perseverance. An *Entertainment Weekly* columnist wrote, "Oliver can get a little overbearing, as even his wife admits, just because he's always so darn earnest."[111]

For Oliver's efforts in improving world health, Harvard University's School of Public Health presented him with its Healthy Cup Award on May 22, 2012. Department of Nutrition chair Walter Willett cited Oliver's "extraordinarily wide-ranging efforts to combat childhood obesity, through your television programs, your foundation, and Food Revolution Day, and your focus on making healthier food available to children in schools and at home."[112]

After launching a string of projects aimed at improving the world's eating habits, Oliver was ready to take a step back from his missionary zeal. While it was far from time to retire, he was ready to move on to other endeavors, including a television collaboration with his best friend from childhood.

Chapter 6

Feeding the Future

After attempting to reform school lunches in England and America, Oliver took a break from his efforts to change the world's eating habits and returned to his core business: launching new TV series and selling cookbooks. By 2012, he had written fifteen books and had appeared in thirteen series. In his 2010 series for England's Channel 4, *Jamie Does*, Oliver traveled to places such as Marrakesh, Morocco; Andalusia, Spain; Stockholm, Sweden; and Venice, Italy. In each of these countries, he put his own spin on some of the local dishes. Along with the series came a cookbook of the same name.

Oliver also launched a series of lunch meals-to-go at Boots, a pharmacy chain in Britain. The meals were traditional English pub favorites, such as the ploughman's lunch (made up of cheeses and cold cuts) and prawn cocktails. However, Jamie trimmed all the meals down to fewer than five hundred calories.

One Meal—Thirty Minutes

Also in 2010, Oliver aired *30-Minute Meals*, his first daytime television series in England. The goal was to show home cooks that they could prepare an entire meal in just thirty minutes, using only ingredients they already had at home. The book that went along with the series became the fastest-selling cookbook to date in England. Oliver became only the second British author of any genre to sell more than £100 million ($152 million) worth of books. The only other person to achieve that status was J.K. Rowling, author of the hugely successful Harry Potter series.

Book sales aside, many reviewers questioned whether Oliver's meals lived up to their promise. Critics were skeptical that an inexperienced cook could really prepare them in thirty minutes or less. Tim Hayward, blogger for the *Guardian* who attempted a vegetable curry from Oliver's TV show, managed to cook the meal in thirty minutes; however, he said

Despite the number of cookbooks Oliver has written, critics have said some recipes are not all that easy to make and some of the ingredients are hard to find.

Is Jamie Oliver Too Fat?

Jamie Oliver has spent much of his career fighting obesity and getting people to eat more healthfully. But in 2012, he was accused of being a hypocrite when photos of him getting off a plane in Australia revealed he had put on some weight. Fellow celebrity chef Gordon Ramsay—who has never hidden his dislike for Oliver—commented that Oliver was too fat to lecture anyone else on weight loss.

When reporters challenged Oliver about his weight gain, he replied, "I do my best. Working in the food business is quite hard when someone is constantly asking you to try things." He affirmed that he eats fresh food and exercises with a trainer twice a week to stay in shape. "I could definitely do better, but I am trying to do my best like most people when they hit 30."

Quoted in Katie Moisse. "Jamie Oliver Defends His Weight." *Medical Unit* (blog) ABC News, March 7, 2012. http://abcnews.go.com/blogs/health/2012/03/07/jamie-oliver-defends-his-weight/.

the resulting product was an "undercooked curry sludge," that took a full forty-five minutes to clean up. "To be honest, the individual details of the ensuing debacle are just too depressing to relate," he wrote. "As the closing credits rolled, my kitchen looked like a crime scene."[113] Hayward's colleague and co-blogger, Susan Smillie, who took more than an hour to assemble a red prawn curry, concluded that "this mid-week 30-minute against-the-clock extravaganza sucked the joy out of cooking for me."[114]

Undaunted by the negative publicity, Oliver aimed for even quicker cooking with his 2012 book *15-Minute Meals*. Whether his meals seemed possible or pleasurable to make in such a short amount of time seemed not to matter to readers: *15-Minute Meals* sold nearly 374,000 copies in England during the Christmas season. This time he overtook Rowling, beating sales of her first adult novel, *The Casual Vacancy* (which sold just under 317,000 copies), to become the top-selling book of the year in England.

Jamie & Jimmy

On a roll, Oliver brought in an old friend when creating his next television project. Oliver and Jimmy Doherty had been pals since childhood. They had gone to school together, traveled on family vacations together, and had often gotten into mischief together. The two men had stayed close through the years, and in 2012, they decided to collaborate on a TV show. Called *Jamie & Jimmy's Food Fight Club*, the show is set at a café that the two friends opened on Southend Pier, a seaside resort in Essex. After producing series after series alone, it was nice for Oliver to finally have a partner. "I have never had anyone to bounce off [of],"[115] Oliver says.

The point of the show is to prove that English food can compete with cuisine from any other country. "Metaphorically speaking, we are standing on the white cliffs of Dover [along England's coast across the channel from France] shaking our fists in the air and saying, 'Come on then, if you think you're hard enough,'"[116] Oliver says of the challenge he and Doherty put out to chefs in other countries. Some of those challenges included trying to brew better beer than the Belgians or to make sausages that rivaled those of the Germans.

Bringing two childhood friends together was bound to lead to some silliness, and *Jamie & Jimmy's Food Fight Club* definitely delivered. "It feels as though we're 12 again, and it has been a right laugh,"[117] Oliver says. "It is the funniest thing I have done in 15 years."[118] In one episode, for example, they gave a spray tan to a circle of Brie cheese. In another, the two men had an argument over Chewbacca, the Wookiee from *Star Wars*. They even challenged actress Gwyneth Paltrow to stuff her mouth full of marshmallows and then try to say, "Chubby bunny." They also challenged each other to eat a burger, fries, and drink a milkshake while riding the pier's rollercoaster. They ended up wearing most of the meal by the end of the ride. "It's quite a frightening rollercoaster and for me it was horrific—there was

Jimmy Doherty and Jamie Oliver have been friends since childhood and collaborated on the English cooking program **Jamie & Jimmy's Food Fight Club.**

food flying everywhere,"[119] recalls Oliver. The craziness might have been fun for Oliver and his pal, but it did not go over well with critics. One called the show "the least intelligible cooking programme in living memory."[120]

Celebrity Chefs

Jamie Oliver is one of many chefs who have parlayed their cooking skills into an empire of television shows, books, and corporate endorsements. Possibly the very first celebrity chef in the United States was Julia Child, who had a highly popular French cookbook and a string of cooking shows from the 1960s to the 1990s.

The modern celebrity chef trend was begun in earnest by Wolfgang Puck when he opened a chain of restaurants in the 1980s. Born in Austria, Puck created the famous Spago restaurant on Los Angeles's Sunset Strip. From there, his empire expanded to include several restaurants, cookbooks, cookware, and a line of frozen foods.

Another beloved celebrity chef is Emeril Lagasse. He was born in Fall River, Massachusetts, but became known for his New Orleans–style cooking and for his enthusiastic use of the catchword "Bam!" Today Lagasse is so recognizable that people know him by first name alone.

Mario Batali brought classic Italian cooking to America with a string of restaurants such as Babbo, Bar Jamon, Del Posto, and Otto. He is also known as one of the Food Network's Iron Chefs and cohosts the ABC daytime talk show *The Chew*.

Finally, Gordon Ramsay is known as the bad-boy of TV chefs. His hot temper is on full display in the series *Hell's Kitchen*, in which he often berates chefs-in-training. Born in Glasgow, Scotland, in 1966, Ramsey established his name by opening a series of respected restaurants around the world.

Julia Child could be considered the first celebrity chef. She had a popular French cookbook and televised cooking shows from the 1960s to 1990s.

New Horizons

Never content to work on a single project, Oliver juggled several new ventures at once. He wrote a book with a companion six-part television show called *Jamie Oliver's Great Britain*, which was an ode to the great pub culture and culinary legacy of his country. In 2013 he lent his fame to the Essex visitor's guide, encouraging tourists to stay and play in the county where he was born.

That same year, Oliver launched his newest YouTube cooking video channel, called Jamie Oliver's Food Tube. On the channel, fans can ask questions, which Oliver answers throughout his live-streamed shows. To celebrate the launch of Food Tube, Oliver pulled a stunt that got him into the *Guinness Book of World Records*. He broke the world record—and proved his superior knife skills—by chopping ten chilies in just thirty seconds. (His competitor, former mentor Gennaro Contaldo, only got through five chilies in the same period of time.)

Cooking Up a Promising Future

In 2012 England's *Sunday Times* newspaper valued Oliver's wealth at a staggering £150 million ($229 million). That made him the richest chef in Great Britain (richer even than Gordon Ramsay—the British chef who stars in several Fox network reality shows), and the second richest author (after Rowling).

Money does not always buy happiness, though. For Oliver, being with his family has always been most important—and he always tries to make time for them. He, Jools, and their four children split their weeks between their London and Essex homes. They spend time in the garden or watching a movie together. "We're just ordinary," he says. "Jools is amazing and I treasure the weekends and our holiday time more than anything."[121] The couple has talked about having more children, but with Oliver's busy schedule that seems uncertain. While Jools kept pushing for a fifth child, Oliver would not give in. "I sort of feel like we are just out of nappies [diapers] now and I have got four kids and it's more than enough," he said in 2012. "It's quite hard to

Oliver remains one of the wealthiest chefs in Great Britain and has managed to fine-tune his work schedule around his family, which he values more than anything.

have time for each other when you have four kids so I don't want another excuse for me and Jools not to have time together."[122] Furthermore, Oliver had finally figured out how to manage his work schedule to spend more time with his family and felt he had achieved a balance he did not want to tinker with further.

As for the future, Oliver plans to "keep doing what I'm doing, raising my family, writing books, making telly [television], and making noise around issues that I believe in,"[123] he says. With no plans to retire and bolstered by an empire of shows, books, restaurants, and products, Oliver has ensured that the world—and its kitchens—have not seen the last of him.

Notes

Introduction: The Crusade Against Turkey Twizzlers

1. Quoted in Lisa Abend. "The Cult of the Celebrity Chef Goes Global." *Time*, June 21, 2010. www.time.com/time/magazine/article/0,9171,1995844-2,00.html.
2. *Lancet*. "Jamie Oliver for Chief Medical Officer?," April 9, 2005, p. 1282.
3. Quoted in Jessica Gunn. "Passing On the Passion." *Caterer & Hotelkeeper*, November 27, 2003, p. 22.
4. Quoted in Bruce Kemble. "Jamie Oliver." *Healthy Eating*, August 1999.
5. Jamie Oliver. *Jamie's Kitchen*. New York: Hyperion, 2003.
6. Quoted in Kemble. "Jamie Oliver."
7. Jay Rayner. "Jamie Oliver. You Might Want to Hate Him, but You Can't Help Cheering." *Guardian* (Manchester, UK), July 5, 2012. www.guardian.co.uk/commentisfree/2012/jul/05/jamie-oliver-cant-help-cheering.

Chapter 1: Pint-Sized Chef

8. Quoted in Kemble. "Jamie Oliver."
9. Quoted in Hannah Nathanson. "My London: Jamie Oliver." *London Evening Standard*, October 8, 2010. www.standard.co.uk/lifestyle/my-london-jamie-oliver-6522640.html.
10. Quoted in Georgia Dehn. "Jamie Oliver: 'Food Was Always a Big Part of My Holidays.'" *Telegraph* (London). www.telegraph.co.uk/culture/tvandradio/9698449/Jamie-Oliver-Food-was-always-a-big-part-of-my-holidays.html.
11. Quoted in Dehn. "Jamie Oliver."
12. Quoted in Jessica Allen. "In Conversation with Jamie Oliver: Why Britain Really Is Great." *Macleans*, October 18, 2012. www2.macleans.ca/2012/10/18/in-conversation-with-jamie-oliver-why-britain-really-is-great/.

13. Quoted in Epicurious.com. “Mother’s Day Recipes from the World’s Top Chefs.” www.epicurious.com/articlesguides/holidays/mothersday/mothersdaychefstories.
14. Quoted in Allen. “In Conversation with Jamie Oliver.”
15. Jamie Oliver. “Happy Days with the Naked Chef: Interview with My Mum.” Jamie Oliver’s webpage on the website of his publisher, Penguin Books Ltd. www.penguin.co.uk/static/cs/uk/0/minisites/jamieoliver/interviewmum.html.
16. Quoted in Dehn. “Jamie Oliver.”
17. Jamie Oliver. *The Naked Chef*. New York: Hyperion, 2000.
18. Quoted in Kemble. “Jamie Oliver.”
19. Quoted in Oliver. “Happy Days with the Naked Chef.”
20. Quoted in Kemble. “Jamie Oliver.”
21. Quoted in Oliver. *The Naked Chef.*
22. Quoted in Oliver. “Happy Days with the Naked Chef.”
23. Quoted in Laura Clark. “Jamie Oliver Sets Up School to Help Youngsters with Dyslexia Reach Their Full Potential.” *Mail* Online, June 17, 2010. www.dailymail.co.uk/news/article-1287158/Jamie-Oliver-set-school-help-youngsters-dyslexia-reach-potential.html.
24. Quoted in Miranda Sawyer. “Dish of the Day.” *Observer* (London), April 13, 2002. www.guardian.co.uk/theobserver/2002/apr/14/features.magazine47.
25. Quoted in Jane Graham. “Jamie Oliver: ‘I’m Much Calmer than the Original Me.” *Big Issue*, January 3, 2013. www.bigissue.com/features/letter-my-younger-self/1819/jamie-oliver-my-voice-shook-when-i-talked-girls-i-sounded.
26. Quoted in Graham. “Jamie Oliver.”
27. Quoted in Mark Jefferies. “Jamie Oliver Admits Jools Dated Him Because She Felt Sorry for Him After He Crashed His Car on Their First Date.” *Mirror* (London), November 9, 2012. www.mirror.co.uk/tv/tv-news/jamie-oliver-admits-jools-dated-1425563.
28. Quoted in Sawyer. “Dish of the Day.”
29. Oliver. *The Naked Chef.*

Chapter 2: Discovery in the Kitchen

30. Oliver. *The Naked Chef.*
31. Quoted in Kemble. “Jamie Oliver.”

32. Quoted in Kemble. "Jamie Oliver."
33. Jamie Oliver. "'I Loved Him from Day One.'" *Guardian* (Manchester, UK), June 10, 2003. www.guardian.co.uk/education/2003/jun/11/furthereducation.uk.
34. Quoted in Kemble. "Jamie Oliver."
35. Oliver. "'I Loved Him from Day One.'"
36. Quoted in Jade Wright. "Greedy Italian Gennaro Contaldo on How He Made Beatles Legend Paul McCartney Sing for His Supper." *Liverpool Echo* (UK), May 10, 2012. www.liverpoolecho.co.uk/liverpool-life/liverpool-lifestyle/2012/05/10/greedy-italian-gennaro-contaldo-on-how-he-made-beatles-legend-paul-mccartney-sing-for-his-supper-100252-30935683/.
37. Michael Bateman. "Food from the River Café: The Tastes of Tuscany." *Independent* (London), April 2, 1995. www.independent.co.uk/arts-entertainment/food-from-the-river-cafe-the-tastes-of-tuscany-1613975.html.
38. Quoted in Kemble. "Jamie Oliver."
39. Quoted in Bruce Palling. "The River Café: Famous Alumni." *London Magazine*, March 28, 2012. www.thelondonmagazine.co.uk/London-Living/More-London-Living/The-River-Cafe-famous-alumni.html.
40. Oliver. *The Naked Chef*.
41. Quoted in Palling. "The River Café: Famous Alumni."
42. Quoted in Elizabeth Jensen. "'Naked Chef' Specializes in Stripped-Down Style." *Los Angeles Times*, October 31, 2000. http://articles.latimes.com/2000/oct/31/entertainment/ca-44477.
43. Quoted in Xanthe Clay. "Jamie Oliver: How the Golden Boy Grew Up." *Telegraph* (London), August 30, 2007. www.telegraph.co.uk/news/features/3633976/Jamie-Oliver-How-the-Golden-Boy-grew-up.html.
44. Quoted in Stephen Armstrong. "Recipe for Success." *Guardian* (Manchester, UK), January 7, 2007. www.guardian.co.uk/media/2007/jan/08/mondaymediasection12.

Chapter 3: Becoming the Naked Chef

45. Quoted in Jensen. "'Naked Chef' Specializes in Stripped-Down Style."

46. "Jamie: The Naked Chef." YouTube, April 11, 2011. www.youtube.com/watch?v=EbgnpQzmbuY.
47. Quoted in Jensen. "'Naked Chef' Specializes in Stripped-Down Style."
48. Quoted in Rick Marin. "Getting Naked with: Jamie Oliver; The Chef Who Turns It Up to 11." *New York Times*, December 17, 2000. www.nytimes.com/2000/12/17/style/getting-naked-with-jamie-oliver-the-chef-who-turns-it-up-to-11.html?pagewanted=all&src=pm.
49. Quoted in Armstrong. "Recipe for Success."
50. Jay Rayner. "Naked Ambition." *Observer* (London), September 16, 2000. www.guardian.co.uk/lifeandstyle/2000/sep/17/foodanddrink.restaurants.
51. Quoted in Graham. "Jamie Oliver."
52. Clay. "Jamie Oliver."
53. Quoted in Rebecca Thomas. "Jamie Oliver's Naked Sounds." BBC Online, April 11, 2000. http://news.bbc.co.uk/2/hi/entertainment/709292.stm.
54. Quoted in Thomas. "Jamie Oliver's Naked Sounds."
55. James Poniewozik. "*The Naked Chef*," *Time*, November 6, 2000. www.time.com/time/magazine/article/0,9171,998452,00.html.
56. Quoted in Andrew Billen. "Jamie Still Shows Naked Ambition." *London Evening Standard*, July 11, 2001. www.standard.co.uk/goingout/restaurants/jamie-still-shows-naked-ambition-6341019.html.
57. Quoted in *People*. "Jamie Oliver: Sexiest Chef," November 13, 2000. www.people.com/people/archive/article/0,,20132912,00.html.
58. Quoted in Billen. "Jamie Still Shows Naked Ambition."
59. Quoted in *People*. "Jamie Oliver."
60. Quoted in *People*. "Jamie Oliver."
61. Quoted in Jane Gordon. "The Next Chapter." *Mail* Online, September 12, 2008. www.dailymail.co.uk/home/you/article-1049389/Just-old-fashioned-girl-Jools-Olivers-chapter.html#axzz2KhMdiwFk.
62. Quoted in BBC News. "Naked Chef Ties the Knot," June 24, 2000. http://news.bbc.co.uk/2/hi/entertainment/803555.stm.

63. Quoted in Sawyer. “Dish of the Day.”
64. Quoted in Armstrong. “Recipe for Success.”

Chapter Four: A Culinary Star with a Good Heart

65. Quoted in Kemble. “Jamie Oliver.”
66. Quoted in Martin Burton. “Jamie Oliver.” *Director*, February 2006.
67. Quoted in Bruce Boyers. “Jamie Oliver: Passionate Casual Caring Revolutionary.” *Organic Connections*, n.d. http://organicconnectmag.com/wp/jamie-oliver-passionate-casual-caring-revolutionary/#.UNB686Vm2n0.
68. Quoted in Gunn. “Passing On the Passion,” p. 22.
69. Quoted in Hardens. “Fifteen,” 2012. www.hardens.com/az/restaurants/london/n1/fifteen.htm.
70. Victor Lewis-Smith. “Fifteen, London N1.” *Guardian* (Manchester, UK), October 22, 2004. www.guardian.co.uk/lifeandstyle/2004/oct/23/foodanddrink.shopping1.
71. Jon Henley. “Jamie Oliver's Fifteen: A Winning Recipe.” *Guardian* (Manchester, UK), April 9, 2012. www.guardian.co.uk/society/2012/apr/09/jamie-oliver-fifteen-winning recipe
72. Matthew Norman. “Restaurant Review: Jamie's Italian.” *Guardian* (Manchester, UK), July 25, 2008. www.guardian.co.uk/lifeandstyle/2008/jul/26/restaurants.review.
73. Quoted on the Union Jacks website. www.unionjacksrestaurants.com.
74. Jay Rayner. “Restaurant Review: Barbecoa.” *Guardian* (Manchester, UK), May 7, 2011. www.guardian.co.uk/lifeandstyle/2011/may/08/jay-rayner-barbecoa-jamie-oliver.
75. Quoted in Kemble. “Jamie Oliver.”
76. Quoted in Alun Palmer. “Jools Wants Another Baby but I'm Hoping for More Date Nights: Jamie Oliver on Fatherhood.” *Mirror* (London), November 24, 2012. www.mirror.co.uk/3am/celebrity-news/jamie-oliver-on-fatherhood-jools-wants-1453068.
77. Quoted in Gordon. “The Next Chapter.”
78. Quoted in “Jamie's Great Italian Escape–E06–Amalfi Part 1.” YouTube. www.youtube.com/watch?v=ElhW4DXQwBY.

79. Quoted in Gordon. "The Next Chapter."
80. Quoted in Gordon. "The Next Chapter."
81. Quoted in Lara Gould. "Jools Doesn't 'Get' What Drives Me: Jamie Oliver Admits His Marriage Isn't Easy Thanks to His Workload." *Mail* Online, September 27, 2011. www.dailymail.co.uk/tvshowbiz/article-2041443/Jamie-Oliver-admits-marriage-isnt-easy-thanks-workload.html#axzz2KhMdiwFk.

Chapter 5: Food Revolution

82. JamieOliver.com. "Jamie's School Dinners." www.jamieoliver.com/school-dinners/.
83. Quoted in John Crace. "Cool Dinners." *Guardian* (Manchester, UK), February 14, 2005. www.guardian.co.uk/society/2005/feb/15/education.schools.
84. Quoted in Crace. "Cool Dinners."
85. Quoted in Crace. "Cool Dinners."
86. Quoted in Boyers. "Jamie Oliver: Passionate Casual Caring Revolutionary."
87. Quoted in Gaby Hinsliff and Amelia Hill. "Blair Acts on Jamie's Plan for Schools." *Observer* (London), March 19, 2005. www.guardian.co.uk/society/2005/mar/20/childrensservices.food.
88. Brendan O'Neill. "Jamie Leaves a Nasty Aftertaste." *New Statesman*, May 8, 2006, p. 18.
89. Quoted in Hinsliff and Hill. "Blair Acts on Jamie's Plan for Schools."
90. Quoted in Abend. "The Cult of the Celebrity Chef Goes Global."
91. Quoted in Crace. "Cool Dinners."
92. Quoted in Chris Druce. "School Dinners and the Jamie Oliver Effect." *Caterer & Hotelkeeper*, October 22, 2010. www.catererandhotelkeeper.co.uk/articles/21/10/2010/335581/school-dinners-and-the-jamie-oliver-effect.htm.
93. Quoted in O'Neill. "Jamie Leaves a Nasty Aftertaste," p. 18.

94. Quoted in *Mirror* (London). "School Sinners," September 16, 2006. www.mirror.co.uk/news/uk-news/school-sinners-641937.
95. O'Neill, "Jamie Leaves a Nasty Aftertaste," p. 18.
96. Quoted in Druce. "School Dinners and the Jamie Oliver Effect."
97. Quoted in Boyers. "Jamie Oliver."
98. Quoted in Jamie Oliver's Kitchen. "The Kitchen Garden Project." www.jamieoliver.com/kitchen-garden-project/kgp.php.
99. Quoted in Matthew Appleby. "School Gardens Next Target for Jamie Oliver." *Horticulture Week*, February 10, 2012. www.hortweek.com/news/1116160/School-gardens-next-target-Jamie-Oliver/?DCMP=ILC-SEARCH.
100. Hank Stuever. "'Jamie Oliver's Food Revolution' Regurgitates the Worst of Reality TV Pap." *Washington Post*, March 20, 2010. www.washingtonpost.com/wp-dyn/content/article/2010/03/19/AR2010031901683.html.
101. Quoted in Stuever. "'Jamie Oliver's Food Revolution' Regurgitates the Worst of Reality TV Pap."
102. "Jamie Oliver's Food Revolution, Episode 1, Part 3." YouTube. www.youtube.com/watch?v=hUuW2_rqEzM.
103. Arun Gupta. "How TV Superchef Jamie Oliver's 'Food Revolution' Flunked Out." AlterNet, April 7, 2010. www.alternet.org/story/146354/how_tv_superchef_jamie_oliver's_'food_revolution'_flunked_out.
104. Quoted in Mary MacVean. "Jamie Oliver's 'Food Revolution' Makes Its Case with Teenagers." *Los Angeles Times*, June 11, 2011. http://latimesblogs.latimes.com/showtracker/2011/06/jamie-olivers-food-revolution-makes-its-case-with-teenagers.html.
105. Quoted in *Daily Mirror* (London). "American School Kids Trash Jamie Oliver's Food Revolution," January 29, 2012. www.mirror.co.uk/news/uk-news/american-school-kids-trash-jamie-658131.
106. Quoted in Boyers. "Jamie Oliver."

107. Stephen Marche. "Is Jamie Oliver the Biggest Loser of All?" *Esquire*, December 14, 2010. www.esquire.com/features/thousand-words-on-culture/jamie-oliver-food-revolution-0111.
108. Quoted in *Huffington Post*. "Jamie Oliver's Food Revolution Day Aims to Inspire 'Better Food, Better Life,'" April 28, 2012. www.huffingtonpost.com/2012/04/28/jamie-oliver-food-revolution-day_n_1461430.html.
109. Quoted in Robin McKie. "Jamie Oliver Calls for Global Action to Tackle Obesity." *Observer* (London), September 3, 2011. www.guardian.co.uk/lifeandstyle/2011/sep/04/jamie-oliver-global-action-obesity.
110. Jamie Oliver. "Food Revolution Day." *Huffington Post*, May 17, 2012. www.huffingtonpost.com/jamie-oliver/food-revolution-day_b_1524926.html.
111. Keith Staskiewicz. "Jamie Oliver's Food Revolution." *Entertainment Weekly*, April 22, 2011, p. 91.
112. Quoted in Harvard School of Public Health. "Jamie Oliver Receives 2012 Healthy Cup Award," May 23, 2012. www.hsph.harvard.edu/news/features/jamie-oliver-healthy-cup-award-html/.

Chapter 6: Feeding the Future

113. Tim Hayward, Tim Lusher, Susan Smillie, and Vicky Frost. "Bish, Bash, Bosh: Putting Jamie's 30 Minute Meals to the Test." *Word of Mouth Blog, Guardian* (Manchester, UK), October 26, 2010. www.guardian.co.uk/tv-and-radio/tvandradioblog/2010/oct/26/jamie-olivers-30-minute-meals.
114. Hayward, Lushner, Smillie, and Frost. "Bish, Bash, Bosh."
115. Quoted in Jefferies. "Jamie Oliver Admits Jools Dated Him Because She Felt Sorry for Him . . ."
116. Quoted in Dehn. "Jamie Oliver."
117. Quoted in Dehn. "Jamie Oliver."
118. Quoted in Jefferies. "Jamie Oliver Admits Jools Dated Him Because She Felt Sorry for Him . . ."
119. Quoted in *Daily Mirror*. "Jools Wants Another Baby . . ."
120. Sarah Dempster. "Jamie & Jimmy's Food Fight Club Is Absolutely Baffling." *Guardian* (Manchester, UK), November

30, 2012. www.guardian.co.uk/tv-and-radio/2012/nov/30/jamie-and-jimmy-food-fight-club-baffling.

121. Quoted in *Cosmopolitan*. "Fun Fearless Male: Jamie Oliver," p. 189.
122. Quoted in Fehintola Betiku. "'I Have Got Four Kids and It's More than Enough': Jamie Oliver Reveals He Doesn't Want Anymore Children." *Mail* Online, November 24, 2012. www.dailymail.co.uk/tvshowbiz/article-2237910/Jamie-Oliver-reveals-doesnt-want-anymore-children.html.
123. Quoted in *Huffington Post*. "Jamie Oliver's Food Revolution Day Aims to Inspire 'Better Food, Better Life.'"

Important Dates

May 27, 1975
Jamie Oliver is born in the village of Clavering, Essex, England.

1991
Oliver drops out of school at age sixteen and attends Westminster Catering College, a London cooking school.

1996
Oliver gets a job at the River Café, working for renowned chefs Rose Gray and Ruth Rogers.

December 1997
A BBC special, "Christmas at the River Café," features a fresh-faced Jamie Oliver in the background. He is noticed and sought out by several television producers.

April 1999
The Naked Chef TV series premieres on the BBC television network in England.

2000
Sainsbury's supermarket chain makes Oliver its spokesperson. Immediately, sales of the products he endorses increase by several hundred percent.

June 24, 2000
Oliver and longtime girlfriend, Juliette (Jools) Norton, get married at a church in Essex, England.

November 2000
The Naked Chef premieres in the United States on the Food Network.

People magazine names Jamie Oliver the "sexiest chef" in its annual "Sexiest Men Alive" issue.

2002

Oliver launches the Fifteen restaurant charity to provide culinary training for at-risk youths.

March 18, 2002

Oliver and his wife welcome their first child, Poppy Honey Rosie Oliver.

April 10, 2003

Second daughter, Daisy Boo Pamela Oliver, is born.

February 2005

Jamie's School Dinners, about Oliver's efforts to reform England's school dinner (lunch) program, premieres on England's Channel 4 television network.

2008

Oliver launches a chain of casual Italian restaurants called Jamie's Italian.

April 3, 2009

Oliver's third daughter, Petal Blossom Rainbow, is born.

March 2010

Jamie Oliver's Food Revolution, about his attempts to change eating habits in America's "fattest" city—Huntington, West Virginia, airs on ABC television.

September 15, 2010

Oliver's son, Buddy Bear Maurice, is born.

May 19, 2012

Oliver launches the first annual Food Revolution Day to get the world talking about more healthful eating.

November 2012

Jamie & Jimmy's Food Fight Club premieres on Channel 4 in England.

2013

Oliver goes live on his YouTube channel, Jamie Oliver's Food Tube, and becomes the face of the Essex visitor guide.

For More Information

Books

Robin Brancato. *Food Choices: The Ultimate Teen Guide (It Happened to Me)*. Lanham, MD: Scarecrow Press, 2010. Readers can learn why people like to eat certain foods and how to improve their own eating habits.

Jamie Oliver. *Jamie's Food Revolution*. New York: Hyperion, 2011. In this book, which is a companion to the TV show of the same name, Oliver teaches readers how to cook simple, healthful meals through a series of easy recipes.

Brandon Robshaw. *Jamie Oliver*. London: Hodder Arnold, 2006. Readers can learn more about the life of celebrity TV chef Jamie Oliver in this easy-to-read biography.

Jodie Shield. *Healthy Eating, Healthy Weight for Kids and Teens*. Chicago: Eat Right Press, 2012. This book teaches teens to navigate the unhealthy world of fast food and how to make better food choices.

Internet Sources

Stephen Armstrong. "Recipe for Success." *Guardian* (Manchester, UK), January 7, 2007. www.theguardian.com/media/2007/jan/08/mondaymediasection/2.

Fehintola Betiku. "'I Have Got Four Kids and It's More than Enough': Jamie Oliver Reveals He Doesn't Want Anymore Children," *Mail* Online, November 24, 2012. www.dailymail.co.uk/tvshowbiz/article-2237910/Jamie-Oliver-reveals-doesnt-want-anymore-children.html.

Andrew Billen. "Jamie Still Shows Naked Ambition." *London Evening Standard*, July 11, 2001. www.dailymail.co.uk/tvshowbiz/article-2237910/Jamie-Oliver-reveals-doesn't-want-anymore-children.html.

Bruce Boyers. "Jamie Oliver: Passionate Casual Caring Revolutionary." *Organic Connections*, n.d. http://organicconnectmag.com/wp/jamie-oliver-passionate-casual-caring-revolutionary/#.UVNSo79gNlI.

Xanthe Clay. "Jamie Oliver: How the Golden Boy Grew Up." *Telegraph* (London), August 30, 2007. www.telegraph.co.uk/news/features/3633976/Jamie-Oliver-How-the-Golden-Boy-grew-up.html.

Georgia Dehn. "Jamie Oliver: 'Food Was Always a Big Part of My Holidays.'" *Telegraph* (London), November 23, 2012. www.telegraph.co.uk/culture/tvandradio/9698449/Jamie-Oliver-Food-was-always-a-big-part-of-my-holidays.html.

Chris Druce. "School Dinners and the Jamie Oliver Effect." *Caterer & Hotelkeeper*, n.d. www.catererandhotelkeeper.co.uk/articles/21/10/2010/335581/school-dinners-and-the-jamie-oliver-effect.htm.

Jane Gordon. "The Next Chapter." *Mail* Online, September 12, 2008. www.dailymail.co.uk/home/you/article-1049389/Just-old-fashioned-girl-Jools-Olivers-chapter.html.

Jon Henley. "Jamie Oliver's Fifteen: A Winning Recipe." *Guardian* (Manchester, UK), April 9, 2012. www.guardian.co.uk/society/2012/apr/09/jamie-oliver-fifteen-winning-recipe.

Elizabeth Jensen. "'Naked Chef' Specializes in Stripped-Down Style." *Los Angeles Times*, October 31, 2000. http://articles.latimes.com/2000/oct/31/entertainment/ca-44477.

Stephen Marche. "Is Jamie Oliver the Biggest Loser of All?" *Esquire*, December 14, 2010. www.esquire.com/features/thousand-words-on-culture/jamie-oliver-food-revolution-0111.

Robin McKie. "Jamie Oliver Calls for Global Action to Tackle Obesity." *Observer* (London), September 3, 2011. www.guardian.co.uk/lifeandstyle/2011/sep/04/jamie-oliver-global-action-obesity.

People. "Jamie Oliver (The Sexiest Man Alive 2000)," November 13, 2000. www.people.com/people/archive/article/0,,20132912,00.html.

Jay Rayner. "Jamie Oliver. You Might Want to Hate Him, but You Can't Help Cheering." *Guardian* (Manchester, UK), July 5, 2012. www.guardian.co.uk/commentisfree/2012/jul/05/jamie-oliver-cant-help-cheering.

Keith Staskiewicz. "Jamie Oliver's Food Revolution." *Entertainment Weekly*, April 22, 2011.

Websites

Fifteen.net (www.fifteen.net) The website of Oliver's flagship Fifteen restaurant describes the charity that teaches young people cooking skills.

Foodnetwork.com (www.foodnetwork.com) The Food Network is home to several of Oliver's cooking shows, as well as shows from other celebrity chefs.

Jamieoliver.com (www.jamieoliver.com) Oliver's own website is an excellent source of news about his television shows, books, and other endeavors.

Jamie Oliver's Food Tube (www.youtube.com/user/JamieOliver) Jamie Oliver's Food Tube channel on YouTube includes live cooking videos from Oliver, to which fans can subscribe.

Index

Picture Credits

About the Author

Stephanie Watson is a writer and editor who lives in Providence, Rhode Island, with her husband and son. She has been writing young-adult nonfiction for the better part of a decade and over that time has written several celebrity biographies, including *Heath Ledger: Talented Actor*, *Daniel Radcliffe: Film and Stage Star*, and *The Earnhardt NASCAR Dynasty: The Legacy of Dale Sr. and Dale Jr.* Stephanie is also a regular contributor to WebMD, and is executive editor of *Harvard Women's Health Watch*. In her free time she enjoys doing charity work and traveling with her family.